5 STEPS

Your Guide to Financial Health

NOW WITH TWO BONUS CHAPTERS

Donald A. Galade

Copyright © 2019 by Donald A. Galade

5 Steps

Your Guide to Financial Health

Now With 2 Bonus Chapters

By: Donald A. Galade

Edited by: Donald J. Galade, Cheryl Galade

All rights reserved. All rights reserved solely by the author. The author guarantees all contents are original and do not infringe upon the legal rights of any other person or work. No part of this book may be reproduced or used in any manner without written permission of the copyright owner except for the use of quotations in a book review. The views expressed in this book are not necessarily those of the publisher.

*Disclaimer: No investment, legal or tax advice is recommended or implied. No advice on specific products, financial vehicles or services are recommended or implied. One should seek qualified estate planners, financial advisors, tax professionals, brokers and/or attorneys when completing a comprehensive estate plan, or depositing money into any savings or investment vehicle. Read all documentation, brochures and prospectus carefully. All Biblical references noted in this work may however be applied to everyday life and used as needed without disclosure!

www.galadefinancial.com

ISBN: 9781794678194

Contents

INTRO:	1
STEP 1: To Save or To Invest?	3
STEP 2: Consider an Annuity	29
STEP 3: Income Planning	50
STEP 4: The Action Plan	59
STEP 5: How to Find the Right Advisor	83
BONUS: The Long-Term Effects	90
7 Major Advance Warnings	105
ABOUT:	i

INTRO:

It's been said that few plan to fail but many fail to plan. Many people do not put the proper time and energy into building a well-balanced financial plan. When planting a garden one must nurture the plants to yield a bountiful harvest. The same is true for your nest egg.

This short book will show the reader how to break down the monumental task financial planning into five easy to manage steps.

Let's go on a journey together, but first we need a map and a plan.

Donald A. Galade

STEP 1:
To Save or To Invest?

In this chapter we will talk about some specific principals in saving and investing. Before we do however, we must define these two terms. Many use them inter-changeably, but they are not the same. Savings is for a short-term goal such as an emergency fund or a vacation. i.e. "I am saving for my vacation in July, or I am saving to buy someone a special present." Investing is indicative of a long-term goal such as a child's education fund or retirement.

When you invest, your time horizon is generally different than when you save. Since your goals are different, you need to place the funds in different vehicles in order to achieve or reach your goal. I will often use the term vehicle to describe a particular investment or savings instrument. For example, if you and I were at the mall and we chose to leave and go to another store, we would get in our vehicles to arrive at our new destination. If I chose to drive a motorcycle and you drove a school bus, we would arrive at our destinations at different times. I would get there faster than you and I would probably take a lot more risk in doing so, thus we used different vehicles to achieve a similar goal. With that being said, you do not place your savings in the same type of vehicles that you would use for investing. Since the required end result is different, the means to the end should be different as well. An example of a savings vehicle would be a certificate of deposit, or a money market account. It is liquid and has no market risk. It does have inflation risk, but that is acceptable since we realize there is no "perfect" vehicle for every goal. An example of an investment vehicle may be a mutual fund or common stock. The time horizon is longer than our savings goal, so we can afford to take some market risk in the hopes of receiving a much higher appreciated account value when we need the funds.

You save for a rainy day, but you invest for the future. Please be sure to match the best vehicle to your goal. Many do not, and they become disappointed when they lose their savings in the market, since this bucket of money was ear-marked for a goal that could not sustain market risk, thus it was inappropriately assigned. Notice I said the assignment was inappropriate, not the investment. You cannot blame the vehicle for "losing money." That's what it is capable of. If you utilize the wrong tool for the job, you cannot blame the tool for the outcome.

The biggest questions we get from those nearing retirement are "Do I have enough money to live on," and "What accounts should I spend first?" Once again, unless you have outlined all of your current savings and investment vehicles and have had a detailed analysis performed on the portfolio, this question does not have a one-size fits all answer.

The average American spends more time planning next year's vacation, or their daughter's wedding than they do building a financial plan. If you decided to build a house, the first thing you would do is have someone draw up a floor plan. From that drawing an architect would draw blue prints. These prints will become the "bible" to the contractor in order to build your dream house. It tells the carpenters where everything goes; the precise measurements of the walls and ceilings, and the types of materials to be utilized in construction. You would never build a house without a blueprint, right? Then why do people invest without a carefully structured plan? The reason is they usually take the advice of many different stock brokers and insurance

STEP 1

sales people, and are not working with a true advisor, let alone someone who specializes in income planning estate conservation.

One must constantly monitor the progress of the plan in conjunction with the long- term goal, not the short-term result in any one year. If you lose sight of the big picture, you may find yourself changing products within your portfolio. Those changes may not be in alignment with your original goals. As the date of your retirement draws closer, you should assume less risk in your portfolio. At this point of your life your focus should switch to conservation of what you have built, and income generation for the rest of your life, rather than capital appreciation. Obviously, you still want your assets to grow, but be sure you are comfortable with the amount of risk you have assumed in retirement years.

Some have a concern about leaving a legacy to the next generation, others do not. Many clients are concerned about minimizing taxes both short term and long-term; all are worried about cash flow, "Will I run out of money before I die?"

A colleague of mine had a client whose goal was to eliminate risk and generate a life- time income. All his assets were subject to risk. At 79 years young, 100 percent of his assets were subject to 100 percent risk. If his goal was truly to generate an income that he could not outlive and eliminate risk, he would have agreed to the recommendation to reallocate monies away from a risk position. He did not heed this advice; thus, he did not implement the strategies prepared for him. In short, he ended up losing 50 percent of his nest egg in retirement years when he needed the income most. He now has less money to leave to his children as a legacy as well. He may never recoup the losses he witnessed in his lifetime, for time is not on his side. His un-teachable spirit caused him to lose the very thing he sought to protect. The market did not let him down; he chose to listen to the wrong advice and utilized the wrong advisor. You may know this advisor, Mr. "don't worry; it's only a paper loss."

Now I ask you, is it his goal or his mindset that needed to be adjusted? He clearly had a well-defined goal, but as I said he had an un-teachable spirit. His mind was made up, and he believed what he was always told. "Stay the course, don't worry it will come back." These adages may be true if you are in your 30's, and can sustain excessive market risk, but when you are 65 staring at retirement in 45 days, you have made some bad personnel decisions with regard to whom you have hired to manage your money. If you had a true financial advisor who built a platform for your portfolio, you would not have excessive risk at this age; and the required vehicles needed to generate the lifetime income you need would have been in place. It's all about the blueprint!

So now where do you actually place your funds? This is the million-dollar question, (pun intended) that I am asked constantly, and the answer is simple. "I can't answer you." I could not give the answer until I had the opportunity to spend some time with the client. We must first identify your goals, income needs, risk tolerance, retirement lifestyle, tax bracket, legacy desires and a few other things. We must also know if you are going at-this alone or with God, for there is a difference in how you will allocate your funds. I have both believers and non-believers as clients. These two groups will approach investing differently.

Sometimes the best advice we can offer a client will not always be received by our client, such as the gentleman I mentioned previously. I often disagree with colleagues of mine when it comes to asset allocation. Not all advisors are the same. Many choose products for a client that may be more in line with the advisors best interests rather than that of the client. One cannot say a particular product is either good or bad for every person. If they did, they are a fool. Not everyone should drive a Buick!

Every vehicle on the market has an expressed designed purpose. If you do not use the vehicle for its designed purpose, you will witness unpleasant results. For example, bonds are generally used as an income producing vehicle, but many purchase them expecting growth. Stock is generally used for long-

STEP 1

term investing and growth, but many retire, or even die with huge portions of their assets at excessive risk, when what they really needed at that time was income. If the adage is buy low and sell high, when do you sell? You plan, that's how.

Types of Vehicles:

Before we talk about what vehicles exist in today's economy, we must discuss some investment mind sets. It is also very important to know exactly where your income stream will come from when you retire. Some investment products have income producing features others do not. Also, you may not be able to convert stocks or bonds to cash as soon as you need income. You may witness some unpleasant results if you liquidate a vehicle at the wrong time. You must also properly assess the tax liabilities that can occur from the sale, and whether the gains or losses are long-term or short term.

The most common type of retirement income stream we see today is that of the traditional pension plan. Although they are rare, some still exist. About 24 percent of Americans will get a traditional pension plan when they retire. These are funds that are set aside by the employer from whom you worked. In most instances all of the proceeds received were derived from your employer's contributions.

The next "bucket" of income we will refer to is Social Security. While the normal age to start collecting full benefits has been pushed back to 67 years for many, you still can take early retirement and collect at age 62, at least for now. The Social Security Administration will send frequent reports on what your benefit will be at the various ages in which you decide to start receiving your checks. I encourage you to visit www.ssa.gov, the official Social Security website, and see what your benefits "will be" before you start to map your trip around the world. Also, many people think that they will gain a large increase in Social Security (SS) payments by delaying benefits for a few years. Although you will see a modest increase in benefits by waiting, don't! I have seen many a 65-year-old die waiting for a small increase in SS benefits. There are a multitude of advisors out there who disagree with this theory. That is just one of the reasons, I am different.

Some use complicated formulas as to pull from their qualified plan now and leave SS benefits until age 70 or longer in the hopes of a larger pay out. Here is a simple rule of thumb, if you need the money now, take it now. This is not rocket science. You should also have a qualified advisor do an analysis of what your survivor benefit would be if your spouse dies before you. In other words, who has the larger SS benefit, and what would my income be when my spouse dies? Knowing that information ahead of time allows you to properly plan. You can ear-mark a certain bucket of money to grow specifically for the replacement of spousal income that will be needed when your spouse passes away. Now your income will be "fixed," but it's fixed at a number that out-paces inflation and covers your income needs!

Taxable accounts: You may have various taxable accounts such as non-qualified annuities, brokerage accounts, mutual funds, statement savings, certificate of deposit, money market, limited partnerships, or bonds, just to name a few. Dealing with the right advisor is important when ascertaining which vehicles should be utilized for income now verses which should be re-allocated into other income producing accounts for the future. Will market exposure and inflation risk play a role in which accounts to spend? How about taxation, do you think it matters? You betcha! Sometimes there are advantages for spending, the non-qualified funds first. Your existing tax bracket is an important factor to consider before liquidation starts.

Do you may have charitable goals? If you chose to leave a portion of your estate to charity, it may make sense to preserve tax-deferred accounts by naming the charity as the beneficiary before you pass away. Accounts with low tax bases can be ear

STEP 1

marked for lifetime charitable gifts to family members in low tax brackets.

If you are dealing with the right advisor, he or she would subscribe to a distribution planning /wealth management software solution. A software solution such as this allows planners the ability to efficiently provide accurate guidance to their clients about complex subject matter such as this. It has the capability to identify multiple distribution strategies. Such a solution can provide a detailed report which shows the full impact of your liquidation choices as well as cash flow, and the long-term impact on estate gifting choices before you implement the technique. It's kind-of like being a Monday morning quarterback on Sunday morning. You got all the data before the game, just run the plays!

Previously I spoke a lot about ways to earn but as the title says, it's what you keep that matters. Even if you had a crystal ball, you would still run the risk of outliving your money if you suffer from a catastrophic illness before you die. Sure, you can buy long-term care (LTC) insurance, but the fact is many people don't. Long-term care (LTC) is the type of care referenced to those who have chronic health conditions or disabilities.

There are three types of care, skilled, intermediate and custodial. This type of care is broken into two distinct categories; nursing home and home health care. The names are self-explanatory as to how the care is received by the medical professionals. Many do purchase this coverage but a few years later they forget why they purchased it and let it lapse, usually right before a long-term illness, which is why they purchased it in the first place. Others look at the cost of the insurance and assume they cannot afford it. In some cases, I agree. If you have a total net worth of $50,000, I do not see long- term care insurance as a real value. If on the other hand your net worth is $750,000, it may be worth it to have this coverage. You would never cancel your homeowners or auto insurance, because you didn't have a fire yet. Well, odds are that many of us will have some sort of long-term care need before we die. Nursing homes are full of the people who said, "I'm never going to a nursing home." That phrase is from your lips to God's ears, for only He knows. If you have saved a sizeable nest egg, you should insure it from the potential loss due to the threat of long-term illness.

No one expects to need this type of care, but we also do not expect a fire in our home or an auto accident, which is why there are insurance plans to cover this type of loss. Statistically 40 percent of us will need this type of care before we meet the Lord face to face, according to the Alzheimer's association's 2010 statistics. 14 percent of people age 71 and older have Alzheimer's disease, a disorder that will require extensive long-term care. Younger people may require this type of care as well. A one-year stay in a nursing facility can cost as much as $75,000. So, the question is, "Should I buy a long- term care policy?" Since Medicare and most Medi-Gap or Medicare Advantage plans do not provide coverage for anything other than 100 days of skilled care, you may want to consider it if you do not wish to pay for the care out of pocket.

The cost of the coverage is driven by your current age and health. The older you are at time of purchase obviously the higher the premium will be. The benefit amount is the maximum the policy will pay over the life of the contract broken down by a daily dollar amount i.e. $150 a day up to a policy max of $50,000. The benefit amount usually has a time frame in which payments will be paid such as two years or three years. Most contracts have an illumination period or a time in which no benefits can be received after illness has commenced. This period is set at inception of the policy as it is directly correlated to the premium. The longer illumination period such as 120 days will have a lower premium. The types of facilities one can receive care in vary. You can have a nurse come to your home thus the name home care. Care can be received in an assisted living facility or a type of facility that simulates your own home and only minimal "assistance" with activities of daily living (ADL's) is required. Then there are

STEP 1

facilities known as adult day care, which is exactly what the name implies, and lastly the nursing home.

Be careful of the company you choose for this coverage. Many smaller health insurance companies have gone out of business because they did not price the coverage to meet the true actuarial costs of this type of care. The cheapest is not always the best. Choose a company that has an A rating or better. Purchase a plan that has an inflation protection rider so that as the costs of the care increases, the coverage does as well. Be sure the plan covers both in-home and nursing home care and make sure it covers all three levels of care: skilled, intermediate and custodial. Not all plans are equal and DO NOT shop for this coverage based on price; you will get what you pay for.

Another option to adequately protect your nest egg from a catastrophic illness and pending financial ruin is a newer type of contract that has a combination of life, LTC and a savings component built in. A client can deposit a lump sum of money into a single premium product such as a life insurance policy or an annuity contract with a participating insurance company. Depending upon the client's age and health, the insurance company issues the contract with a pre-determined death benefit and a long-term care benefit accordingly. No future premiums are added to the contract. In the event of a catastrophic illness, the contract pays for the long-term care need. If no illness arises, the funds can be withdrawn at a later date as a return of premium feature with a modest interest rate attached, or simply left in reserve with the insurance company to be utilized as a death benefit after the person passes away. Some may witness added tax benefits from this type of plan.

This contract acts like an annuity, has a death benefit provision, and has LTC benefits all in one policy. In the future if you wanted to pullout your cash, you can. In the event you died without a LTC illness, your beneficiaries get the proceeds, but if you got sick, the contract has a pre-determined LTC pay-out provision. For example, say you had $150,000 you wanted to protect. Your advisor can split funds into two separate single premium contracts, each funded with $75,000 one for each spouse. You can then elect benefit of two times the coverage level, so that each contract provides $150,000 of LTC coverage. In this case the fixed deferred annuity will credit each contract approximately 2.32 percent tax-deferred in 10 years. More importantly, you have turned your $150,000 in premium into $300,000 in funds to pay for long-term care expenses tax-free under the Pension Protection Act. In the event you do not need to utilize the LTC benefit the funds can pass the death benefit (which differs on all policies, this example is merely illustrative) to your heirs and in many instances avoid probate.

This is just one way to protect yourself from spending all your cash with on care or insurance. You must implement such a plan when you are young and healthy, so do not procrastinate!

Many base their retirement solely on the amount of funds they have before they retire. I present to you that there are many factors to consider before you tell your boss you plan to quit work. You must consider the amount of debt you have at retirement age. Factors such as how you will pay for your health insurance, how will inflation affect your funds, and do you have other sources of income besides your retirement account must be applied?

Retiring With Too Much Debt: If you have excessive debt, it will be more difficult to sustain your current life style. Feeding the beast takes food off the table.

Inadequate Insurance: At age 65 you qualify for Medicare, but Medicare alone does not pay for all your health care needs. A supplement must be purchased in order to complete your health coverage. Many retire without exploring the costs associated with this coverage.

STEP 1

Ignoring Inflation and Market Risk: Inflation will slowly have a negative impact upon your nest egg. Retiring with too much market risk can also be detrimental to your expectation of a life income.

Relying Too Heavily on One Income Source: Generations before us worked a single job their entire life. Unfortunately, many find they must continue to work or return to the work force after they retire for a myriad of reasons. Conversely many retire dependent upon one income source. For example: Let's say you are dependent upon dividend income from your portfolio to meet your monthly needs. As you know, dividends are not guaranteed. If the dividend paying stock you are relying on suddenly stops paying its dividend, you could suddenly find yourself saying "paper or plastic," against your will.

Too Much Invested and Not Enough Saved: As discussed previously, a savings account is different than an investment. If you need a new roof, a new car, or suddenly have a great deal on that dream vacation, you should have a pool of money to pull from that will not affect your income stream. Many keep all their funds in the same bucket, and simply withdraw money as needed for all needs. This is likened to a sailor spending his pay while on shore-leave. You need to allocate funds into specific buckets. If you simply withdraw money from the "same" account for everything, you run a high risk of over-spending or outliving your money.

According to a recent ING survey, many workers (87 percent) said they could be saving more in their employer-sponsored retirement plan, a savings vehicle they deem critically important to reaching a secure retirement, and the foundation of most of their retirement savings strategy. In fact, of the 1,000 workplace retirement plan participants surveyed, nearly two-thirds (64 percent) said their employer-sponsored retirement plan accounts for all or most of their retirement portfolio. However, many participants are not stretching to maximize their contributions when they can. Moreover, they tend to rely on "guesswork" when setting contribution levels, and don't fully understand the importance and long-term impact of small increases in contribution rates. *

"Americans today understand that they shoulder a greater responsibility for securing their own retirement," said Rob Leary, CEO, ING Insurance U.S. "They also recognize that an employer-sponsored retirement plan is the cornerstone of their efforts to save for retirement. Still, the issue for many workers, made even more urgent in shaky economic times and an era of volatile equity markets, is scrubbing household budgets and, when possible, finding more dollars to save for retirement. Being cost-conscious is certainly important and prudent, but at the same time, people must also find ways to contribute more into their retirement accounts."

Retirement plan funding agreements issued by ING Life Insurance and Annuity Company ("ILIAC") One Orange Way, Windsor, CT 06095, which is solely responsible for meeting its obligations. Plan administrative services provided by ILIAC or ING Institutional Plan Services, LLC. Securities distributed by or offered through ING Financial Advisors, LLC (member SIPC) or other broker-dealers with which it has a selling agreement. All companies are members of the ING family of companies. SOURCE ING Copyright (C) 2010 PR Newswire. All rights reserved.

The basic component to measure growth in any vehicle is its interest rate. Compounding interest calculations may be somewhat of an enigma to some. The chart below illustrates how a $2,000 investment can grow over a period of time if it received a five percent annual rate of return.

STEP 1

Starting Age	Invested Yearly	Total Invested	5% Return at 65
18	$2000	$94,000	$378,134
25	$2000	$80,000	$378,134
40	$2000	$50,000	$99,450
50	$2000	$30,000	$44,637

Notice how a small amount of $2,000 per year can grow to a healthy sum over a longer period of time, even at a conservative interest rate. Also notice the cost associated with waiting. The person who began investing at age 18 has more resources than the person who waited until he was 50 to start investing. You do not have to be an investment banker with an MBA in economics to generate a sizeable nest egg as you reach the golden years. You simply need to implement a plan and have the tenacity to stick to it.

Now let's review the same example as above except this person is going to invest $5,000 a year, and for this example we will again use a five percent return annually. Note this is not illustrating a specific investment. The illustration is merely used to show time value of money using different rates of return.

Starting Age	Invested Yearly	Total Invested	5% Return at 65
18	$5000	$235,000	$1,824,754
25	$5000	$200,000	$1,091,922
40	$5000	$125,000	$336,989
50	$5000	$75,000	$131,856

Notice that with a $3,000 per year increase in deposits accompanied by a more attractive rate of return, a younger person can be a millionaire at age 65 if he or she simply saves on a consistent basis. This sounds good on paper, but it will not work unless you actually implement the plan (and receive the rate depicted in the example, of course). Keep in mind that this does not include taxation or inflation. Obviously, the net amount would be substantially less when we factor these components into the mix.

This illustration was meant as a simple guide to show how money can accumulate using basic interest calculations. To illustrate how much you would need to save to retire with the same life style you currently have, we generally utilize a complex computer pro- gram that takes into consideration all variables such as income needs, risk tolerance, taxation, life expectancy, and potential market corrections and exposure, and the potential need for long-term care medical expenses.

As mentioned above, inflation is a factor that can affect your end result and must be taken into consideration as you set up your plan. I have included a simple illustration to show how inflation can plague your portfolio. In this example, we will demonstrate the effect inflation has on your nest egg. If you had $1,000,000 in 1965 you would need $6,728,824.28 in 2009 to have the same purchasing power. Now let's look at this equation in reverse. A home purchased in 1965 for $145,545.64 would cost $1,000,000 in 2009. So, you can see you will need more assets in retirement years just to sustain the same lifestyle you currently have.

This chart shows historical inflation rates from 1920 to 2010. Notice that we are actually witnessing one of the lowest inflationary periods in our country's history. There is a storm on the horizon in my opinion, and inflation will not remain this low for an extended period of time.

STEP 1

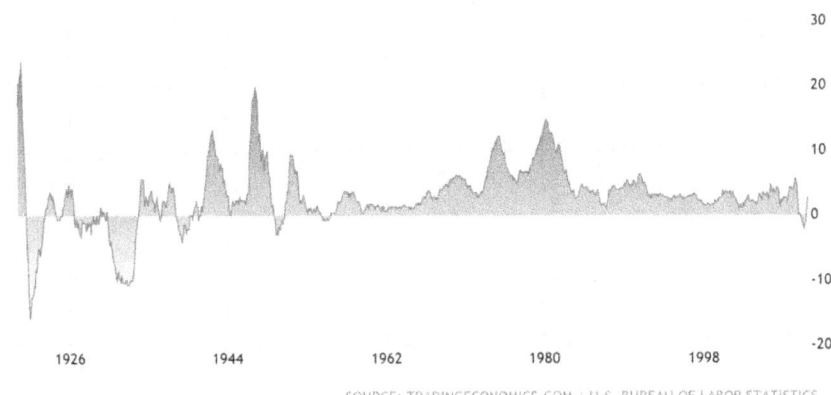

Tax rates must increase to satisfy the growing national debt. There is no way for our government to pay its current debt under the current administration without an increase in taxation, or "revenue enhancement" as it is now called. The National Debt is at a level that has never been witnessed before. The economy as well as the markets will eventually react to this indebtedness.

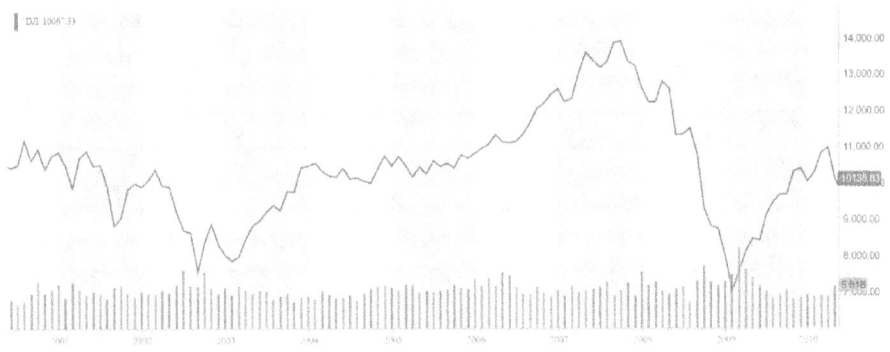

Source: Yahoo Finance

As you can see our current tax brackets are actually at near historical lows thus, as discussed, an increase is imminent given the economic climate we are in currently, coupled with the size of the mounting national debt.

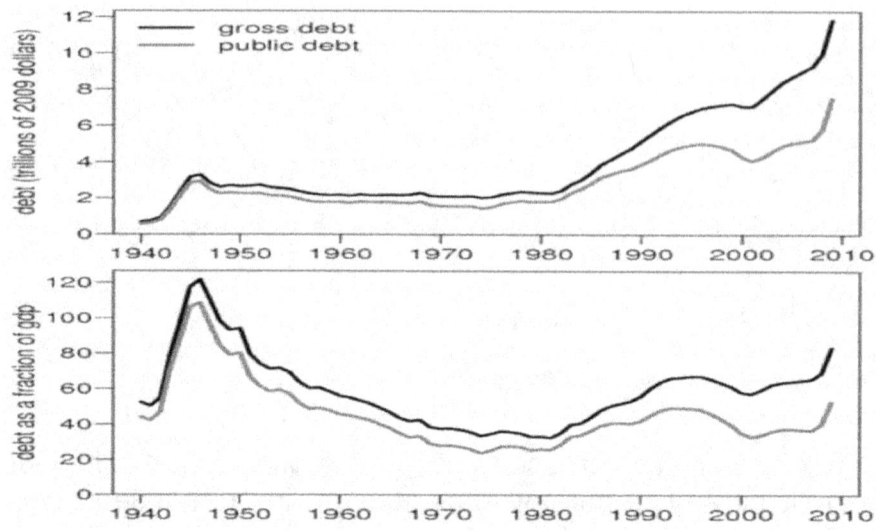

Source: Wikipedia: http://en.wikipedia.org/wiki/United_States_public_debt.

Data on our national debt is changing every second. I invite you to visit the website: www.usdebtclock.org. for an updated real-time snapshot of our current debt.

I encourage everyone to read a series of books by author Ed Slott. Mr. Slott is a CPA and world-renowned author on IRAs and taxation. Ed Slott is a non-biased resource to use when generating an income, estate, and tax plan. In other words, he's not trying to sell you anything; it's just good advice. Mr. Slott talks in detail about converting your traditional IRA to a ROTH IRA. This may or may not be in your best interest. There are a few factors that you need to address before you pull the switch on this transaction.

According to Ed Slott:

Taxes on high-income individuals and trusts will be increasing in 2011-2012 and again in 2013 when the 3.8 percent and .09 taxes become effective. Planning needs to begin NOW to prepare

STEP 1

for future tax increases, especially for tax-payers and trusts at the top tax brackets.

IRA and plan distributions are exempt from the 3.8 percent surtax on net investment income, but taxable distributions from them can push income over the threshold amounts causing other investment income to be subject to the tax.

2010 Roth conversions are now more valuable as a means to eliminate future taxable income and eliminate future Required Minimum Distribution or RMDs, from traditional IRAs before higher tax rates become effective.

Taxpayers that have named a discretionary trust as their beneficiary should consider Roth conversions to avoid potential harsh trust tax rates at low trust income levels.

Salary deferrals (401(k), 403(b), etc.) can reduce the Modified Adjusted Gross Income or MAGI, for the 3.8 percent surtax but cannot reduce earned income for the .09 percent additional Medicare tax.

Trusts will be hit particularly hard as the 3.8 percent surtax kicks in at much lower income levels. (Trust threshold by 2013 will be approximately $12,000).

Source https://www.irahelp.com/

Some think that if they have not converted a traditional IRA into a ROTH IRA before 2010, that the opportunity is gone. That is far from the truth. In some instances, it is still a very viable option. Many are unaware that the ROTH conversion can also be used in conjunction to offset other taxable events or losses. For example, if you have a variable annuity that is "under water" or witnessing a loss you may use this opportunity to get out of that product and offset the losses against a ROTH conversion of another traditional IRA. Obviously, this is just mentioned as a concept, and expert tax advice should be secured before making such a bold move. If you were a farmer would you want to pay tax on the "seed" or the "harvest"? Think of that analogy as you contemplate a ROTH conversion.

IRA/ROTH/401(k):

Many people saving for retirement use a qualified plan such as an IRA, 401(k), TSA or 403(b) plans. The word "qualified" means that the plan gets preferential tax treatment. Most qualified plans are held by individuals who are between 40-79 years old. This is virtually the entire baby boomer generation. Once an individual reaches age 70½ they must take funds out of the IRA, or qualified plan, as part of a required minimum distribution. The purpose for the mandatory withdrawal is to provide tax revenue for Uncle Sam. If a qualified plan did not have mandatory withdrawal provisions, a recipient could pass untaxed proceeds of the plan to another person upon their demise without paying taxes. Such an action would prove to be unprofitable for the government.

People often get confused between the type of program they have, such as an IRA, 403(b) or 401(k) plan and the vehicles that actually cause their plan to make or, in some instances lose money. Implemented in 1974, the IRA is commonly referred to as an Individual Retirement Account, but actually it is an Individual Retirement Arrangement. Many think 401(k) or IRAs are a "type of investment". That is not true. The name 401(k) and IRA are merely names for the IRS tax code that defines how these plans operate. Your money is generally in a vehicle such as a certificate of deposit, mutual fund, stocks or bonds within the 401(k) or IRA.

In other words, your IRA did not lose money; the investments inside your IRA lost money. Think of your IRA as a car. Products such as annuities or certificates of deposit are types of engines for the car. If you changed from a plan that was funded by an annuity to a plan that was funded by a certificate of deposit, you still have the same car, you just changed engines.

STEP 1

As funds are deposited into qualified plans such as an IRA, the recipient receives a tax deduction from his or her reportable income. The funds within the plan grow tax-deferred, which means you do not pay income tax on the growth until you withdraw your money. Taxes that would normally be due on the growth as the plan accumulates interest are deferred until a future date. For example: If you earned $50,000 a year, and deposited $4,000 into an IRA, you would deduct $4,000 from your earned income as reported to the IRS for that year. Whatever interest that $4,000 earned within the IRA will grow tax-deferred, until it is withdrawn. At that point, because you received a tax deduction for the deposit previously, 100 percent of the funds are reportable in the year it is received.

As you grow older and eventually retire, in theory you would make less money and be in a lower tax bracket, thus as you withdraw the funds and pay the taxes due, the rate of taxation would be less than you are paying currently. Sounds good, right? That was the initial thinking when our government set up these provisions, except now the market is in turmoil, inflation is looming on the horizon, and the government is about to raise the income tax levels to epic proportions to cover the huge debt. It is not as awesome as it was designed to be.

When you reach age 70½, you are forced to withdraw some funds out of your qualified plan so Caesar can get what is his, the taxes. This is what is commonly referred to as a Required Minimum Distribution or RMD. The RMD is calculated using a sliding scale which increases slightly each year after you turn 70½.

If taxes are going up as you withdraw your funds from your IRA or other qualified plan, you will actually pay more tax than you had anticipated when you deposited your hard-earned money into this plan over the past 20 years or more. Your IRA should actually be titled in two names. You and the United States department of the Treasury, for technically they will share in a large portion of the funds you have invested for retirement.

Many IRA owners do not need immediate income but are required to take required minimum distributions. Just because you retired does not mean your money should. If you go fishing you throw the small ones back in the hope of catching a bigger prize. If you do not need the small "RMD", you can utilize those funds to generate a death benefit which will offset potential estate taxes. This is called an IRA or insurance arbitrage. The RMD is utilized to pay for a life insurance premium that can be held in an insurance trust for your heirs. Do not think estate planning is only for the wealthy, and do not procrastinate!

Unfortunately, many will not be insulated from the ever-increasing tax bite of a traditional IRA. Taking RMD's when you do not need the income causes taxation on money you do not currently need. Many will reinvest the funds withdrawn from the IRA after paying the applicable taxes. This converts funds that were previously tax-deferred to a taxable status. The percentage of funds that must be withdrawn to satisfy the RMD's increases as you get older. The unwanted distributions can potentially put a client in a higher income tax bracket or in some instance cause Social Security to become taxable.

ROTH IRA:

Implemented in 1997, as introduced by Senator William Roth of Delaware, a ROTH IRA is different from a traditional IRA in that the deposits placed into the ROTH are NOT deducted from the individual's income tax return, like that of a traditional IRA. All proceeds withdrawn from the ROTH are Tax-Free however if held inside the plan for five years before withdrawal. Standard 59½ rules also apply. For tax year 2011 most people under the age of 50 who earn less than the maximum limit can contribute a maximum of $5,000 per year to a Roth IRA.

One of the hottest topics of 2010 was the Roth conversion. Congress had given us this one-year window where virtually everyone qualified to convert IRA money from its current "tax-

STEP 1

deferred" status to Roth status. Previously you could only convert if your income was below $100,000 annually. On the surface, the idea of turning your IRA into a big pot of tax-free money must sound like a good idea, especially if you listen to many in the industry that make it sound so simple and irresistible. Well, maybe it is. You may still convert an IRA to a ROTH IRA but there are several issues to consider. Don't forget, while all future income and growth on ROTH funds are income tax free, you need to pay income tax now on the money you convert. Now let 's look at whether or not conversion is right for your family. Simply put, you are never required to take any withdrawals from your Roth account and, if you are married, your spouse is not either, even after you pass away. Your ROTH money can grow fully tax-free for the rest of your life.

When your children (or grandchildren, if you wish) inherit this Roth money, they are required to start a minimum annual distribution, but it is based on their age. All future growth continues to be income tax free. You can create an enormous tax-free income legacy for your family. All you must do is write the income tax check now. Sounds easy, right? Before you convert your IRA to a ROTH you must first consider the tax bracket of the surviving spouse who is most likely the beneficiary of the proceeds.

If the beneficiary 's future tax bracket is going to decrease, then it may not be in your best interest to convert. If a charity is the ultimate beneficiary of the plan, it is likely not in your best interest to convert. If you anticipate having a taxable estate a conversion to the Roth IRA will reduce estate taxes. Beneficiary arrangements over-ride wills and divorce decrees. Be sure you review the beneficiary designation regularly so that your hard-earned money goes to the people you want after your demise. Be sure to ask your advisor for a "Legacy Planning Kit" and go through the information with him/her.

If you have many write-offs for the current tax year, it may be a good year to convert. If your modified adjusted gross income

(MAGI) plus one half of your Social Security exceeds $32,000 (married filing jointly) or $25,000 (single) then 50 percent of the Social Security amount over $32,000 ($25,000) will be taxed. If this is the case the RMD from the traditional IRA can cause your Social Security to be taxable, whereas tax free ROTH distributions will not.

It is generally best to pay the taxes due on the conversion from assets outside the IRA. All things being equal tax-free growth is better than taxable growth. A ROTH conversion is generally suitable if legacy planning, tax implications and income needs are addressed prior.

Though the two-year payment disappeared in 2010, converting a traditional IRA to a ROTH may still be a viable solution, depending upon your current income level. First, let's look at whether or not conversion is right for you. It is, after all, your money. If you are under age. So, I think the decision is easy; do it. Just thinking about the number of years your money can grow tax free is enough to make you want to party, and enough to make the IRS queasy! As you start to approach retirement, or if you are already retired, it takes some thought. I like to ask the question, "Will your IRA money be "live it" money or "leave it" money?" If you will be drawing income from your traditional IRA money in retirement, ROTH conversion is probably not for you. Frankly, it will be difficult for you to save on taxes going forward more than you will pay in taxes up front. If, however, your traditional IRA money will most likely be untouched and left to your heirs, ROTH conversion is very attractive. When you turn age 70½ you will need to start required minimum distributions as determined by the IRS on the traditional IRA. You are literally forced by law to start taking taxable distributions and continue them in increasing amounts for the rest of your life. There is no required minimum distribution requirement on ROTH accounts while you, the owner, are alive. Here is where you save every year on taxes and justify the upfront tax expense. After you return to the Lord, your heirs do have to take RMD's, but the distributions are not taxable.

STEP 1

There is yet another strategy to accomplish a similar result of a ROTH conversion. If you use the RMD to purchase an appropriate amount of life insurance, you can pass on converting your IRA money to ROTH and leave a pot of taxable money and a pot of tax-free money to your children when you die. Your beneficiaries can choose how to use both accounts based on their financial situations. That required minimum distribution that you don't need currently can be put to better use. Here's the bottom line: the decision to convert to ROTH is a complicated one that is unique to every individual and family situation. You need to consult with an advisor and tax specialist who are well qualified to ask you the right questions and do the calculations necessary to clearly show you the benefits, and costs, of your decision. You need an expert who will be with you throughout the process whom you are comfortable with. Please, don't do this alone. The benefits are great, but so are the potential pitfalls if done improperly.

The 401(k):

A 401(k) plan is: A defined contribution plan offered by an employer to its employees, which allows employees to set aside tax-deferred income for retirement purposes, and in some cases, employers may match their contribution dollar-for-dollar. Taking a distribution of the funds before a certain specified age will trigger a penalty tax. The name 401(k) comes from the IRS section describing the program. An employer protects against judiciary liability under ERISA code 404-c by offering sufficient education to employees so that the employees can make informed decisions on their 401(k) choices. The rule states that the plan should offer the employee three portfolios to choose from and should give the employee the option to change the allocations within the plan at least on a quarterly basis.

A 401(k) works differently than an IRA. A 401(k) is an employer-sponsored plan. Unlike the IRA, which is funded with money that has already been taxed (your net pay) and an income tax deduction is witnessed on the funds, a 401(k) is deducted from your pay pre- tax. In other words, the money is deducted from your gross pay, thus you have postponed the taxable event until you take the money out, or like the IRA until you are 70½ and you must withdraw the RMD.

When setting up a 401(k) plan with your employer, please do not accept financial advice from your human resource person unless that individual is truly a licensed financial professional. Many trust their employer for financial planning and the employer may not be qualified to perform such a task for you. The employer's representative obviously may have your best interest at heart, so they want you to "max out" your earnings potential in the retirement plan. They may not fully understand the funds and risks associated with their particular plan.

You are considered conservative if you are unwilling to take on market risk; thus, you are willing to forgo market potential in order to achieve safety of principal. You are considered moderately conservative if you can tolerate some volatility, but you are still adverse to short-term downside fluctuations.

You are considered moderate if you are willing to make the volatility vs. potential trade off relative to inflation. This is the most common category among pre-retirees.

You are moderately aggressive if you are willing to take on more downside risk but expect growth when the market rises. And lastly, you are aggressive if you have a tolerance and are willing to stand for unusually longer time frames and extreme volatility.

What is your risk tolerance? If you do not know you are in great danger. Your portfolio may have some excessive risk that you are unwilling to accept. Until you define how much risk you are willing to take and compare it to how much risk you currently have; your portfolio is out of balance with your goals.

So where do I put my money? As mentioned, the financial world has a plethora of choices where one can place his or her money, from cash and cash equivalents to equities. Before you appropriate funds to an investment or a savings plan, you must first assign that money with a specific goal. There is no way to gauge growth unless you have a specific time frame to measure it against. In other words, what was my return over the past five years? Therefore, a goal should be fixed to each asset you have ear-marked as an investment or a savings plan.

In their simplest form, one can break down products into two categories. Equity vehicles, or those products that may be traded on the stock exchange and have an element of market risk, and fixed interest vehicles such as CD's, money market accounts, statement and passbook savings, fixed annuities, and government securities such as T-bills, notes and bonds.

Equities can witness ample growth, but as mentioned, they are subject to risk when the market witnesses a correction. This can be problematic if the market tanks before you need the money, say at retirement. Fixed vehicles generally offer a lower rate of return but have no market risk associated with their growth. There may be inflation risk or interest rate risk associated with some products, so please be sure you understand all types of risk and how it can affect your end result.

Many feel they have a diversified portfolio because they own many different funds. If an individual has all his or her assets subject to risk in the equities class, it does not matter how many different funds are owned, they are not diversified. True diversification means your risk is spread out. It does not mean the number of institutions or accounts you have among several different asset and risk classes. If your advisor has done his/her job properly, he has targeted your goals, and has outlined your applicable risk tolerance.

Now you are ready to start a properly executed financial plan. For instance, your children's education funds will generally be needed in a period of 18 years or less; thus, a vehicle such as a mutual fund may suffice for this goal. Mutual funds are designed to be held for a longer period. Some equity type mutual funds may be a wise choice for retirement funds as well depending upon your risk tolerance. Risk tolerance simply means, how much risk are you willing to take with your principal in order to obtain future growth?

Along the journey, some tweaking of your portfolio will be required. Be cautious of an advisor who suggests frequent trading within an account if your goal is long-term growth. In some instances, buy and hold may be the key for long-term success. The strategy you implement should depend upon the time horizon of when you will need the income. In other words, when will you need to utilize the money?

If set up properly, an estate plan can be free from probate taxes. Probate is one of the death taxes in place in many states. For modest-sized estates, probate costs little. Many advisors use probate as a scare tactic to sell annuity products. Probate may be a real concern to some, but it has a bad reputation caused by many in the insurance industry, since life insurance and annuity contracts automatically pass outside a will and avoid pro- bate. You may avoid probate by transferring assets to a revocable living trust, titling assets as joint tenancy with right of survivorship; designate a beneficiary or "payable-on-death" (POD) provision for savings and CD's. Mutual funds can utilize a "transfer-on-death" (TOD) provision to acquire the same result.

You can also avoid probate by giving assets away while you are alive. Your will has a person named to be your executor. This is the person whom you chose to settle your estate. The executor's duties will be to find and collect all assets including those who owe you money, create an inventory of all assets and appraising them, give notice to creditors such as credit card companies or banks, pay taxes and other debts, and distribute assets according to your will. If you die without a will or a named executor, the state will appoint someone to settle your estate.

STEP 2:

Consider an Annuity

Annuities may be a good vehicle to use for your "safe" money. They come in many flavors and they are defiantly not all created equal. There are four main types I will discuss in this chapter. These vehicles are heralded by some as the vehicle which saved their nest egg from market loss, while others refer to them as the "red-headed" step child of the industry. Like all products we have discussed thus far, not every solution will fit every person's need. For some, annuities work well as a "bond alternative" or income producing vehicle. For others, they may not work well. These contracts may be suitable for a portion of the asset portfolio for those who want to avoid market risk and are in retirement or nearing retirement age*.

*Buyer's Guide to Equity-Indexed Annuities-Used with permission from Cheryl Moore. www.theannuitynerds.com. Prepared by the National Association of Insurance Commissioners-Presented Courtesy of AnnuityNerds.com.

The National Association of Insurance Commissioners is an association of state insurance regulatory officials. This association helps the various insurance departments to coordinate insurance laws for the benefit of all consumers.

This Guide has been written to help you understand annuities in general and equity- indexed annuities. There are different kinds of annuities. It is important for you to understand the differences among various annuities, so you can choose the kind that best fits your needs. At the end of this Guide are questions you should ask your agent or the company. Make sure you are satisfied with the answers before you make a purchase.

What is an Annuity?

An annuity is a series of income payments made at regular intervals by an insurance company in return for a premium or premiums you have paid. The most frequent use of income payments from an annuity is for retirement. An annuity is neither a life insurance nor a health insurance policy. It is not a savings account or a savings certificate. You should not buy an annuity for short-term purposes.

What Are the Different Kinds of Annuity Contracts?

Individual or Group

An individual contract covers only one or two persons. A group contract covers a specific group of people, for example, the employees of an employer.

Immediate or Deferred

An immediate annuity begins to make income payments soon after you pay the premium. The income payments from a deferred annuity start later, often many years later. Deferred annuities have an "accumulation" period, which is the time between when you start paying premiums and when income payments start. The time after income payments start is called the "payout" period.

Single Premium' or Installment Premium

STEP 2

You pay the insurance company only one premium for a single premium annuity. You pay for an installment premium annuity through a series of payments. There are two kinds of installment premium annuities. One kind is a flexible premium contract. You can pay as much as you want, whenever you want, within set limits. The other kind is a scheduled premium contract, which specifies how much your premiums will be and how often you will pay them.

Fixed or Variable

During the accumulation period of a fixed deferred annuity, premiums (less any applicable charges) earn interest at rates set by the company or in a way spelled out in the annuity contract. The company guarantees that it will pay no less than a minimum rate of interest. During the payout phase, the amount of each income payment you receive is generally set when the payments start and does not change. During the accumulation period of a variable annuity, premiums (less any applicable charges) are put into a separate account of the insurance company. You decide how those premiums will be invested, from stock or bond mutual fund choices. The value of the separate account, and therefore, the value of your variable annuity, varies with the investment experience of the funds you choose. There is no guarantee that you will receive all your premiums back. There is also no guarantee that you will earn any return on your annuity. During the payout period of a variable annuity, the amount of each income payment you receive may be fixed (predetermined) or variable (changing with the value of the investments in the separate account).

What Are Equity-indexed Annuities?

An equity-indexed annuity is a fixed annuity, either immediate or deferred, that earns interest or provides benefits that are linked to an external equity reference or an equity index. The value of the index might be tied to a stock or other equity index. One of the most commonly used indices is Standard & Poor's 500 Composite Stock Price Index (the S&P 500), which is an equity index. The value of any index varies from day to day and is not predictable. When you buy an equity-indexed annuity you own an insurance contract. You are not buying shares of any stock of index. While immediate equity-indexed annuities may be available, this Buyer's Guide will focus on deferred equity-indexed annuities.

How Are They Different from Other Fixed Annuities?

An equity-indexed annuity is different from other fixed annuities because of the way it credits interest to your annuity's value. Some fixed annuities only credit interest calculated at a rate set in the contract. Other fixed annuities also credit interest at rates set from time to time by the insurance company. Equity-indexed annuities credit interest using a formula based on changes in the index to which the annuity is linked. The formula decides how the additional interest, if any, is calculated and credited. How much additional interest you get and when you get it depends on the features of your annuity.

Your equity-indexed annuity, like other fixed annuities, also promises to pay a minimum interest rate. The rate that will be applied will not be less than this minimum guaranteed rate even if the index-linked interest rate is lower. The value of your annuity also will not drop below a guaranteed minimum. For example, many single premium annuity contracts guarantee the minimum value will never be less than 90 percent of the premium paid, plus at least 3 percent in annual interest (less any partial withdrawals). The guaranteed value is the minimum amount available during a term for withdrawals, as well as for some annuitization (see "Annuity Income Payments") and death benefits. The insurance company will adjust the value of the annuity at the end of each term to reflect any index increases.

STEP 2

What Are Some of the Contract Features?

Two features that have the greatest effect on the amount of additional interest that may be credited to an equity-indexed annuity are the indexing method and the participation rate. It is important to understand the features and how they work together. The following describes some other equity-indexed annuity features that affect the index-linked formula. Since new equity indexed annuity products are being developed, the contract you are interested in may contain a feature that is not discussed in this Buyer's Guide. If this is the case, ask your agent for an explanation that you understand.

Indexing Method

The indexing method means the approach used to measure the amount of change, if any, in the index. Some of the most common indexing methods, which are explained more fully later, include annual reset (ratcheting), high-water mark and point-to-point.

Term

The index term is the period over which index-linked interest is calculated. In most product designs, interest is credited to your annuity at the end of a term. Terms are generally from one to ten years, with six or seven years being most common. Some annuities offer single terms while others offer multiple, consecutive terms. If your annuity has multiple terms, there will usually be a window at the end of each term, typically 30 days, during which you may withdraw your money without penalty. For installment premium annuities, the payment of each premium may begin a new term for that premium.

Participation Rate

The participation rate decides how much of the increase in the index will be used to calculate index-linked interest. For example, if the calculated change in the index is 9 percent and the participation rate is 70 percent, the index-linked interest rate for your annuity will be 6.3 percent (9%x 70% = 6.3%). A company may set a different participation rate for newly issued annuities as often as each day. Therefore, the initial participation rate in your annuity will depend on when it is issued by the company. The company usually guarantees the participation rate for a specific period (from one year to the entire term). When that period is over, the company sets a new participation rate for the next period. Some annuities guarantee that the participation rate will never be set lower than a specified minimum or higher than a specified maximum.

Cap Rate or Cap

Some annuities may put an upper limit, or cap, on the index-linked interest rate. This is the maximum rate of interest the annuity will earn. In the example given above, if the contract has a 6 percent cap rate, 6 percent, and not 6.3 percent, would be credited. Not all annuities have a cap rate.

Floor on Equity Index-Linked Interest

The floor is the minimum index-linked interest rate you will earn. The most common floor is 0 percent. A 0 percent floor assures that even if the index decreases in value, the index-linked interest that you earn will be zero and not negative. As in the case of a cap, not all annuities have a stated floor on index-linked interest rates. But in all cases, your fixed annuity will have a minimum guaranteed value.

Averaging

In some annuities, the average of an index's value is used rather than the actual value of the index on a specified date. The index averaging may occur at the beginning, the end, or throughout the entire term of the annuity.

Interest Compounding

Some annuities pay simple interest during an index term. That means index-linked interest is added to your original premium amount but does not compound during the term. Others pay compound interest during a term, which means that index-linked interest that has already been credited also earns interest in the future. In either case, however, the interest earned in one term is usually compounded in the next.

Margin/Spread/Administrative Fee

In some annuities, the index-linked interest rate is computed by subtracting a specific percentage from any calculated change in the index. This percentage, sometimes referred to as the "margin," spread," or "administrative fee," might be instead of, or in addition to, a participation rate. For example, if the calculated change in the index is 10 percent; your annuity might specify that 2.25 percent will be subtracted from the rate to determine the interest rate credited. In this example, the rate would be 7.75 percent (10% - 2.25% = 7.75%). In this example, the company subtracts the percentage only if the change in the index produces a positive interest rate.

Vesting

Some annuities credit none of the index-linked interest or only part of it, if you take out all your money before the end of the term. The percentage that is vested, or credited, generally increases as the term comes closer to its end and is always 100 percent at the end of the term.

How Do the Common Indexing Methods Differ?

Annual Reset

Index-linked interest, if any, is determined each year by comparing the index value at the end of the contract year with the index value at the start of the contract year. Interest is added to your annuity each year during the term.

High-Water Mark

The index-linked interest, if any, is decided by looking at the index value at various points during the term, usually the annual anniversaries of the date you bought the annuity. The interest is based on the difference between the highest index value and the index value at the start of the term. Interest is added to your annuity at the end of the term.

Point-to-Point

The index-linked interest, if a n y, is based on the difference between the index value at the end of the term and the index value at the start of the term. Interest is added to your annuity at the end of the term.

What Are Some of the Features and Trade-offs of Different Indexing Methods?

Generally, annuities offer preset combinations of features. You may have to make trade-offs to get features you want in an annuity. This means the annuity you choose may also have features you don't want.

STEP 2

Features	Trade-Offs
Annual Reset	
Since the interest earned is "locked in" annually and the index value is "reset" at the end of each year, future decreases in the index will not affect the interest you have already earned. Therefore, your annuity using the annual reset method may credit more interest than annuities using other methods when the index fluctuates up and down often during the term. This design is more likely than others to give you access to index-linked interest before the term ends.	Your annuity's participation rate may change each year and generally will be lower than that of other indexing methods. Also, an annual reset design may use a cap or averaging to limit the total amount of interest you might earn each year.
High-Water Mark	
Since interest is calculated using the highest value of the index on a contract anniversary during the term, this design may credit higher interest than some other designs if the index reaches a high point early or in the middle of the term, then drops off at the end of the term.	Interest is not credited until the end of the term. In some annuities, if you surrender your annuity before the end of the term, you may not get index-linked interest for that term. In other annuities, you may receive index-linked interest, based on the highest anniversary value to date and the annuity's vesting schedule. Also, contracts with this design may have a lower participation rate than annuities using other designs or may use a cap to limit the total amount of interest you might earn.
Point-to-Point	
Since interest cannot be calculated before the end of the term, use of this design may permit a higher participation rate than annuities using other designs.	Since interest is not credited until the end of the term, typically six or seven years, you may not be able to get the index-linked interest until end of term.

37

What Is the Impact of Some Other Product Features?

Cap on Interest Earned

While a cap limits the amount of interest you might earn each year, annuities with this feature may have other product features you want, such as annual interest crediting or the ability to take partial withdrawals. Also, annuities that have a cap may have a higher participation rate.

Averaging

Averaging at the beginning of a term protects you from buying your annuity at a high point, which would reduce the amount of interest you might earn. Averaging at the end of the term protects you against severe declines in the index and losing index-linked interest as a result. On the other hand, averaging may reduce the amount of index-linked interest you earn when the index rises either near the start or at the end of the term.

Participation Rate

The participation rate may vary greatly from one annuity to another and from time to time within a particular annuity. Therefore, it is important for you to know how your annuity's participation rate works with the indexing method. A high participation rate may be offset by other features, such as simple interest, averaging, or a point-to-point indexing method. On the other hand, an insurance company may offset a lower participation rate by also offering a feature such as an annual reset indexing method.

Interest Compounding

It is important for you to know whether your annuity pays compound or simple interest during a term. While you may earn less from an annuity that pays simple interest, it may have other features you want, such as a higher participation rate. If there is a product feature that you do not understand, ask your agent. If you still do not understand, send the company a letter telling them that you want a written response, so you can study their reply. You will be doing yourself a service!

Can I Take My Money out During the Term?

In most cases, you can take all or part of the money out of a deferred annuity at any time during the term. There may be a cost if you do. Sometimes the cost is a stated dollar amount. In other cases, you give up index-linked interest on the amount withdrawn. Some annuities do not let you make a partial withdrawal until the end of a term.

What Will It Cost Me to Take My Money out Early?

If you withdraw all or part of the value in your annuity before the end of the term, a withdrawal or surrender charge may be applied. A withdrawal charge is usually a percentage of the amount being withdrawn. The percentage may be reduced or eliminated after the annuity has been in force for a certain number of years. Sometimes the charge is a reduction in the interest rate credited to the annuity. Some annuities credit none of the index-linked interest or only part of it if you take out all your money before the end of the term. The percentage that is vested, or credited, generally increases as the term comes closer to its end and is always 100 percent at the end of the term.

Is There Always a Charge to Take My Money out Early?

Your annuity may have a limited "free withdrawal" provision. This lets you make one or more withdrawals without charge each year. The size of the free withdrawal is limited to a set percentage of your annuity's guaranteed or accumulated value. If you make a larger withdrawal, you may pay withdrawal charges. You may also lose index-linked interest on amounts you withdraw. Most annuities waive withdrawal charges on withdrawals made within a set number of days at the end of each term. Some annuities waive withdrawal charges if you are confined to a nursing home or diagnosed with a terminal illness. You may, however, lose index-linked interest on withdrawals.

Are Dividends Included in the Index?

Depending on the index used, stock dividends may or may not be included in the index's value. For example, the S&P 500 is a stock price index and only considers the prices of stocks. It does not recognize any dividends paid on those stocks.

What Are Some Other Equity-indexed Annuity Contract Benefits?

Annuity Income Payments

One of the most important benefits of deferred annuities is the right to use the value built up during the accumulation period to provide income payments during the payout period. While income payments are usually made monthly; you can often choose more or less frequent payments. The size of income payments is based on both the accumulated value in your annuity and the annuity's "benefit rate" that is in effect when income payments begin. The insurance company uses the benefits rate to compute the amount of income payment it will pay you for each $1,000 of accumulated value in your annuity. The benefit rate usually depends on your age and sex, and the form of annuity payment you have chosen. You can usually choose from many forms of annuity payments. You might choose payments that continue if you live, or if either you or your spouse lives, or payments that continue for a set number of years.

Death Benefit

Annuities provide a variety of death benefits. The most common death benefit is either the guaranteed minimum value or the value determined by the index-linked formula.

Tax Deferral

Federal income tax on interest accumulated in an annuity is deferred until you take the interest out of the annuity. You may be required to pay taxes then on the tax-deferred accumulation. You may have to pay a tax penalty if you withdraw the accumulation before you are age 59½. The advantage of tax deferral is that you will probably be in a lower tax bracket in retirement then while you are employed. Also, during the accumulation period, you will be earning interest on money that you would otherwise have used to pay taxes. Tax-qualified annuities are subject to different rules. In any case, you should consult your own tax advisor.

How Do I Know if an Equity-indexed Annuity is Right for Me?

The questions listed below may help you decide which type of annuity, if any, meets your retirement planning and financial needs. You should consider what your goals are for the money you may put into the annuity. You need to think about how much risk you're willing to take with the money. Ask yourself:

- How long can I leave my money in the annuity?
- What do I expect to use the money for in the future?
- Am I interested in a variable annuity with the potential for higher earnings that are not guaranteed and willing to risk losing the principal?
- Is a guaranteed interest rate more important to me, with little or no risk of losing the principal?

- Or, am I somewhere in between these two extremes and willing to take some risks?

How Do I Know Which Equity-indexed Annuity is Best for Me?

As with any other insurance product, you must carefully consider your own personal situation and how you feel about the choices available. No single annuity design may have all the features you want. It is important to understand the features and trade-offs available, so you can choose the annuity that is right for you. Keep in mind that it may be misleading to compare one annuity to another unless you compare all the other features of each annuity. You must decide for yourself what combination of features makes the most sense for you. Also, remember that it is not possible to predict the future market behavior of an index.

STEP 2

Questions You Should Ask Your Agent or the Company

- What is the guaranteed minimum interest rate?
- What charges, if any, are deducted from my premium?
- What charges, if any, are deducted from my contract value?
- How long is the term?
- What is the participation rate?
- For how long is the participation rate guaranteed?
- Is there a minimum participation rate?
- Does my contract have a cap?
- Is averaging used? How does it work?
- Is interest compounded during a term?
- Is there a margin, spread, or administrative fee? Is that in addition to or instead of a participation rate?
- Which indexing method is used in my contract?
- What are the surrender charges or penalties if I want to end my contract early and take out all my money?
- Can I get a partial withdrawal without paying charges or losing interest? Does my contract have vesting?
- Does my annuity waive withdrawal charges if I am confined to a nursing home or diagnosed with a terminal illness?
- What annuity income payment options do I have?
- What is the death benefit?

Final Points to Consider

It is very important that you choose an annuity that you understand well. The purpose of this Buyer's Guide is to help you to understand your annuity. Your agent or insurance company can guide you. Remember that the quality of service you can expect from the company and the agent should also be important to you when you buy an annuity. When you receive your contract, read it carefully. It may offer a "free look" period for you to decide if you want to keep the contract. Ask your agent or insurance company for an explanation of anything you don't understand. If you have a specific complaint or can't get the answers you need from your agent or company, contact your state insurance department.

Guarantees based on the claims paying ability of the issuing insurance company. **Warning:** *annuities are only appropriate for money you cannot afford to lose. Accordingly, annuities should only be used with money to provide income throughout your retirement years, or for funds that must be there for your heirs. Annuities are not appropriate for everyone. Those who wish to subject all their retirement savings and future income potential stock market losses should consider annuities. Annuities provide guaranteed minimum rates of return and should not be considered when return on investment is not desired. Annuities should be used by persons addicted to the adrenaline rush caused by the market panic and equity market calamities. Annuities will not provide the stimulus considered by those who are likely to spend all their savings in short period of time without concern for future needs. (Annuities are long term vehicles that are designed to provide a stream of income over the entirety of a person's life and should not be used by those who wish to run out of money in retirement.) Annuities may not be appropriate for people, who have excess guaranteed retirement income from other sources including company pensions and/or Social Security.*

STEP 2

Guaranteed Income for Life

The US Government Accountability Office recently issued its report that encourages retirees to invest in annuities to assure guaranteed income for life. The report also encouraged the adoption of policies to promote the growth of annuities. US investors have assumed more risk as employers abandoned the traditional pension plan that guaranteed income for life in favor of 401K plans and other defined contribution plans, according to the GAO report. The GAO found that most retirees rely primarily on Social Security and ignore options that guarantee additional lifetime retirement income. Most people who retired with a pension plan received or deferred lifetime income benefits. Conversely, the report found that only 6 percent of those with a 401K or other defined contribution plan chose or purchased an annuity at retirement. The GAO made proposals to encourage the availability of annuities in defined contribution plans. This was also the focus of a congressional hearing earlier this year analyzing the use of annuities in employer plans.

Compliments of www.annuitynerds.com

Standard and Poor's, began rating insurance companies in the mid-1980s, assesses a company's Claims-Paying Ability–that is, its financial capacity to meet its insurance obligations. S&P forms its opinion by examining industry-specific risk management factors, operating performance, and capitalization. Industry-specific risk addresses the inherent risk in and diversity of the insurance business being underwritten. Management factors include how management defines its corporate strategy and the effectiveness of its operations and financial controls. Operating performance focuses on a company's trend for current and future earnings. For capitalization, S&P looks at the company's capital structure, its ability to raise capital, liquidity, and cash flow.

Donald A. Galade

Contact: Standard and Poor's, 55 Water St., New York, NY 10041.

DISCLAIMER: The insurance company rating information changes often and without notice. The ratings shown may not be correct. You are strongly advised to contact the three rating agencies (A.M. Best, S&P, and Moody's) to obtain the current rating for any insurance company. Additionally, this information is not to be considered a recommendation to purchase an annuity, nor a contract or offer to contract, nor is it intended to create public interest in the sale of annuities. You should carefully consider whether any annuity is suit- able to your situation and consult with your own financial planner, legal, and/or tax advisors.

A.M. Best's credit ratings are independent and objective opinions, not statements of fact. A.M. Best is not an Investment Advisor, does not offer investment advice of any kind, nor does the company or its Ratings Analysts offer any form of structuring or financial advice. A.M. Best's credit opinions are not recommendations to buy, sell or hold securities, or to make any other investment decisions.

A.M. Best receives compensation for interactive rating services provided to organizations that it rates. A.M. Best may also receive compensation from rated entities for non-rating related services or products offered by A.M. Best. A.M. Best does not offer consulting or advisory services. For more information regarding A.M. Best's rating process, including handling of confidential (non-public) information, independence, and avoidance of conflicts of interest, please read the A.M. Best Code of Conduct.

STEP 2

Rank	A.M. Best	Standard & Poor's	Moody's
1	A++ Secure/ Superior	AAA Extremely Strong	Aaa Exceptional
2	A+ Secure/ Superior	AA+ Very Strong	Aa1, Aa2, Aa3 Excellent
3	A Secure/ Excellent	AA Very Strong	A1, A1, A3 Good
4	A- Secure/ Excellent	AA- Very Strong	Baa2, Baa2, Baa3 Adequate

Risks

There are several types of risk associated with investing. Many only consider market risk while building a financial plan.

Liquidity Risk

Investors typically will have limited opportunities, if any to redeem their equity-linked CDs prior to maturity. Moreover, the financial institutions do not guarantee the existence of a secondary market. Many equity-linked CDs do not permit the early withdrawal of your investment without the consent of the financial institution. If you need to withdraw your investment before the CD matures, you will incur withdrawal penalties. You also will lose any interest that you would accrue in a regular CD that has the same terms. There is no exception for CDs held in either a traditional IRA account or a Coverdell Education Savings Account (CSA). Therefore, you should carefully consider your retirement needs or the educational needs of a beneficiary of a CSA before investing in equity- linked CDs. Other equity- linked CDs allow for redemption only on pre-specified redemption dates. Therefore, you may not be able to redeem your equity-linked CD when you may want or need your money to be available.

Market Risk

If the equity-linked CD is sold before maturity, it may be worth less than its purchase amount or face value. The equity-linked CD will be subject to several variables, including stock market volatility and changes to the components of the linked index. In addition, there is no guarantee of principal return unless the investment is held to maturity.

Call Risk

An equity-linked CD may be callable. If an equity- linked CD is called, the investor's return may be less than the yield for which the CD would have earned had it been held to maturity. The investor also may not be able to invest their funds at the same rate as the original CD.

FDIC Insurance

In general, equity-linked CDs are insured by the FDIC up to the amount permitted by law. FDIC insurance covers the principal of, and any guaranteed interest on, the equity- linked CDs. Investors should carefully read the issuer's disclosure about how the FDIC limits apply in specific circumstances. Investors also may want to review the FDIC's brochure entitled "Your Insured Deposits."

STEP 2

Calculation of Return

Many financial institutions calculate the return on an equity-linked CD by averaging the closing price of the underlying index over a specific period, rather than simply using the closing price upon maturity of your CD to compute your gain or loss. For example, a financial institution may use an average based on the closing price of the S&P 500 every six months during the term of the CD. The formulas used to calculate your return may lessen the impact of a declining market. However, if the market moves steadily upward during the period that you hold the CD, your return may be significantly less than the index's gain during this period.

Source: https://www.sec.gov/

Please read all brochures and dis- claimers carefully before you decide to utilize any financial vehicle in your portfolio.

STEP 3:

Income Planning

Expenses	$	Expenses	$	Expenses	$
Mortgage/Rent		Medical		Bank Fees	
Gas/Oil/Electric		Dr.Co-pays		Brokerage	
Water/Sewage		Vet		Loans	
Phone/Cable		Subscriptions		Credit	
Appliance		Magazines		Postage	
Maintenance		Memberships		Charges	
Improvements		Groceries		Alimony	
Dental Insurance		Clothing		Charity	
Emergency		Supplies		Tithing	
Auto Loan		Cleaning		Gifts	
Auto Insurance		Eating Out		Disability	
License Fees		Entertainment		Education	
Life Insurance		Personal Items		Gas	
Investment		Hobbies		Repairs	
Health Insurance		Travel		Fees	
LTC Insurance		Books/Movies		Misc.	
TOTALS:		TOTALS:		TOTALS:	

A budget itemizing your expenses is crucial prior to calculating your income needs. Many people may have a budget itemizing their basic income versus expenses, and although that may have been enough in the asset building phase of your life, a more complete budget is needed to assure you are protected from outliving your assets in retirement years. Not all senior Wal-Mart greeters take that job because they like people; Some need the money! I have included a sample of what I would call a detailed budget for your review. Notice the detail given to items many people do not think of as expenses.

Leaving a Legacy

Since everyone would like to be remembered, I propose the question: "What is it you would like to be remembered for?" Obviously, it is nice to leave a six or even seven-digit legacy to your loved ones, but is that most important? I say no! Previously, we mentioned the concept of an Ethical Will. Let your children and grandchildren know what it is that makes you tick while you are alive. You can even set up a video camera in front of the love seat and tell your story on tape. This will generate a video message that can be preserved for generations to come, or even shared on line. The best part is that it is in your own words. That is especially helpful if you cannot type or hand write your message. Following those precepts can sow the seed of eternal life to your heirs. In this chapter we are going to address the financial aspects of leaving a legacy.

Over the next decade or so, experts believe approximately $25 trillion in wealth will be transferred from the elder parents of the baby boomer generation. This will represent the largest intergenerational wealth transfer in history.

Source: The Allianz American Legacies Study

The study consisted of a partnership between Allianz Life insurance company, and Dr. Ken Dychtwald, Ph.D., President of Age Wave and Harris Interactive® Dr. Dychtwald designed the study while Harris Interactive conducted the survey. A random sampling of baby boomers and their parents were asked to identify how they define leaving a legacy.

The objective of the study was to quantify the hopes, fears, priorities, and motivations related to the passing of assets between the two generations.

(For more information about The Allianz American Legacies Study, please visit https://www.allianzlife.com)

Many are uncomfortable with discussing the topic of "leaving" an inheritance, but they are comfortable with talking about the idea of leaving a "legacy." Although you may be talking to your parents about this, you probably are not having a "real" conversation about it. You may even be the one child your parents turn to for all decisions, say the "first born."

Some are comfortable with leaving a slightly larger portion of an estate to the child who has "done the most" for mom and dad in their golden years. I suggest you seek a Christian advisor who has great listening and communication skills to assist you with the "wealth transfer" options.

You can sow a seed of eternal life to your heirs with proper guidance. In this chapter we are going to address the financial and spiritual aspects of leaving a legacy. A well-designed estate plan will allow your assets to pass to the next generation with potentially mitigated estate and income tax consequences. There is a difference between income tax evasion and tax avoidance.

Proper planning serves a purpose in this regard. Many insurance organizations have solution-based programs that assist clients in attaining their goals. The purpose of a program such as this is to address the common issues that plague individuals as they develop their estate plan. Many people do not know who to contact or even realize they have an estate issue often until it is too late. Ask your advisor about this plan.

At the sake of being cliché; No one plans to fail but many have failed to plan. The chart below shows famous Americans who did

STEP 3

not do proper estate planning. Notice the individuals on this list. Many were financially astute, but just did not know of the estate settlement woes or just did not get around to it.

NAME	GROSS ESTATE	TOTAL SETTLEMENT	NET ESTATE	SHRINK RATE
Frederick Vanderbilt	$76,838,530	$42,846,112	$33,992,418	56%
Howard Gould	$67,535,386	$52,549,682	$1,498,704	78%
Al Jolson	$43,851,473	$1,349,066	$3,036,077	31%
John D. Rockeffeler Sr.	$26,905,182	$17,124,988	$9,780,194	64%
Walt Disney	$23,004,851	$6,811,943	$16,192,908	30%
J.P. Morgan	$17,121,482	$11,893,691	$5,227,791	69%
Alwin C. Ernst, CPA	$12,642,431	$712,411	$5,518,319	56%
Elvis Presley	$10,165,434	$7,374,635	$2,790,799	73%
Dean Witter	$7,451,055	$1,830,717	$5,620,338	44%
Gary Cooper	$4,948,985	$1,520,454	$3,454,531	31%
Cecil B. DeMille	$4,043,607	$1,396,064	$2,647,543	38%
Clark Gable	$2,806,526	$1,101,038	$1,705,488	44%
Franklin D. Rooselvelt	$1,940,999	$574,867	$1,366,132	30%
Humphrey Bogart	$910,146	$274,234	$635,912	30%
W.C. Fields	$884,680	$329,793	$554,887	37%
Marilyn Monroe	$819,176	$448,750	$370,426	55%

Bill and Martha Swanson met in 1935. They were childhood sweethearts. They have three children and nine grandchildren. At a recent family function, the oldest son, Billy Jr., stated how much he loved the family homestead. The discussion continued as to what would happen to this property once mom and dad had passed. The other two siblings joined in with their desires to possess this property as well. It became abundantly clear to this family that no thought had been given to what would become of their possessions after they passed away. Bill and Martha did not even have a will, yet alone well-designed estate documents. Their daughter Julie, who is a registered nurse, asked her parents if they had provisions in place such as a long-term care policy, in the event one or both of her parents became seriously ill or incapacitated. The answer there was also an astounding

NO! They did not have power-of-attorney (P.O.A.) documents. Suddenly, it was apparent to the entire Swanson family that their parents' affairs were far from "in order," and work was needed to address these issues.

Many families do not have this conversation until it is too late. I encourage parents and children to discuss "end of life issues" while you are living, as uncomfortable as this may be. Having the proper documentation prior to meeting the Lord can assure less strife and conflict among those left behind.

STEP 3

The Big 5

There are five major estate planning documents you need to have in place prior to your demise:

1. Durable Power-of-Attorney (DPOA)
2. Advanced medical directives, sometimes known as a living will, or "do not resuscitate" order also known as a (DNR)
3. Will
4. Letters of instruction
5. Living Trust (if applicable)

A Durable Power-of-Attorney for healthcare DPAHC/healthcare proxy is a common document used at this stage of life. Be sure you fully understand what it is and is not designed to do before implementing. Execution of the DPAHC is flexible and can be used any time you become incompetent. It is not practical in the event of an emergency since your representative must be present to act on your behalf, and some states do not permit its use.

A Living Will allows you to convey decisions regarding your care without relying on anyone, however, they can generally only be used when you are terminally ill or injured or in a vegetative state. They are usually used to make decisions regarding life sustaining treatments. Emergency medical professionals cannot withhold emergency care based on a living will. Like the DPAHC, some states do not allow their use.

Many confuse a living will with a living trust. Although both are very important estate planning documents; they are quite different. A living will allow you to manage your health-care decision when you become incapacitated; where as a living trust lets you manage your property once incapacitated. A living will is not really a will, but a document that becomes effective when you cannot make decisions for yourself. The living trust is a document that owns your property and at time of need a successor steps up to maintain the operation of said property. It can be set up to be revocable or irrevocable. Many use these terms intermittently and it should not be done so accordingly.

A "Do Not Resuscitate" or (DNR) order allows you to decline heroic measures; which is a loosely defined term, such as CPR if you stop breathing. It is effective in an emergency if the doctor has the DNRF information referenced in your medical chart. If you are not hospitalized at time of need you can wear an ID bracelet or Medic Alert™ necklace or carry a card in your wallet. The downside is like other documents described in this chapter they are not permitted in all states, and there are restrictions to its use for care other than declining CPR.

A Durable Power-of-Attorney (DPOA) allows you to control who acts upon and what they can do with your real property. They are inexpensive to implement and decrease the amount of court intervention that can take place. Like other documents discussed thus far, they are not recognized in all states. Durable power-of-attorney is also misconstrued with power-of-attorney. A POA allows someone to act for you, who need not be an attorney. The durable power creates an agency relationship which remains silent even if you become incapacitated. This makes the durable POA an important estate planning tool.

The durable power ends at death. Be sure you know what you have and or what your needs are in this as in every other instance referenced in this book.

So how does one protect their property? A great question that does not have a one size fits all answer. You can explore a living

STEP 3

trust. A trust is a document that transfers ownership of your property while you are alive to an entity known as a trust, thus get- ting it out of your name. The living trust may survive your death and avoid legal recourse, but they are not cheap.

A second type of transference is a standby trust. A standby trust is like the living trust except the transfer of property does not take place until you become incapacitated. It too can outlive you, but is expensive, and in all situations, many are not recognized in every state.

In some instance an individual can own property jointly. This allows another individual to have immediate access to the asset. Although many implement such an arrangement it is not always advisable. The co-owner's access to the property may not always be a good idea. You may lack the ability to direct the co-owner's actions in your best interest, and when you die the property will pass proportionality to the co-owners. This can be problematic in the event of more than one sibling who may not be listed as an owner. It can also cause an issue if your co-owner pre-deceases you. In days gone by it was a way to shield assets from a nursing home. You heard the proverbial stories of "the house in my kid's name so the nursing home can't get it." Those days are gone forever, but many still use this type of planning. In my opinion this is not planning it's just something Aunt Millie suggested and since she is cheaper than a paid professional you listened. Remember you get what you pay for in life, so don't take short cuts with estate planning! Also remember that any property held jointly with a spouse automatically passes to the spouse upon the first person's demise and qualifies for the unlimited marital deduction. That benefit does not exist when you name anyone other than a spouse as a co-owner. Also think carefully about holding title to property in other forms than jointly with a spouse, (such as you own a vacation property without your spouse) in such a case that property does not get preferential tax treatment under the applicable exclusion amount allowed by law upon the death of the first spouse.

When mom or dad can no longer perform activities of daily living, they will require some assistance. Generally, once activated, that assistance need will progress to a larger need. The transformation from healthy functional senior American to a person who requires 24 hour a day care can escalate quickly. As it does, you may be concerned with mom and dad's welfare that you tend to overlook the financial implications. Do not wait until the need is present to implement your exit strategy. The fire escape is always clearly marked in the blueprints of the building for a reason.

If the person who needs this type of care is a veteran or the spouse of a veteran who served our country during a time of war, they may be eligible for a benefit offered through the Veterans Administration known as the Aide and Attendance benefit. Contact your advisor for details.

Please advise the executor and your family members of the location of all estate planning documents in order to simplify the task of executing them when needed. We will not unpack all these items as I am not an attorney, nor is it my intent to give legal advice. I suggest you find a qualified elder law attorney. Acquire a professional who is truly a specialist in this area and can help you with the necessary documentation needed for your estate plan. In addition to the basic trust(s) referenced thus far, there is a plethora of complex estate planning vehicles at your disposal today.

Before you start dividing up your assets to your children while you are alive, you must be assured that you will have more than enough income to last the rest of your life. I have witnessed instances where parents gave away assets to their children prematurely and soon regretted it because they lived too long and ran out of money. You must ascertain your asset values and net worth.

STEP 4:

The Action Plan

If you have an aging parent there are several things you need to know before they require extensive long-term care: First you need to have the conversation with your parents on this topic. Yes, it is uncomfortable to discuss, but remaining silent to satisfy your emotions will not remove the potential outcome if they get sick. Ask your parents what their wishes are in the event they become incapacitated, or what is the real fear associated with becoming dependent. They may be resentful toward you for inferring they will need this care, but rest assured it's mainly since everyone is reluctant to become a burden on their children. Ascertain their medical care decisions, living arrangements and financial needs, and expectations for when this time comes.

Explore the option of a personal care or assisted living facility before they require the care. I encourage visiting the assisted living facilities and personal care homes in your area long before you need one. This way you have an idea of what type of facility would meet their needs and the cost associated with the care in advance. This is yet another part of the "family meeting" we discussed previously.

Prepare a personal data record to log your conversations after the lines of communication are opened. Review banks accounts, wills, living wills, and power-of-attorney documents with the right professionals. Also, be sure you know the location of these documents in the event they need to be executed after mom or dad is cognitively impaired.

It is obvious that you will need the assistance of a qualified advisor and legal representative who know the laws and restrictions of all the aforementioned documents in the state which you reside. These topics are challenging and may bring up hard feelings or other emotions that may not be pleasant to discuss, especially among family members who would rather burry their head in the sand rather than burry their loved one.

No one enjoys planning, but all who have planned enjoy! It is often easier to broach these topics when you are in the company of an individual who is not "blood related."

Now get the entire family together for lunch. Explain the goal of the meeting and generate an outline of items to discuss in order to keep everyone on topic. You can choose a time when the family will be together such as a holiday or special event but be sure to let the family members who will be involved know this is a business meeting not a social gathering. Save the fellowship for afterwards.

Some people may already have an estate plan that was generated 20 years ago and do not see an inherent need to conduct this meeting. That document from 20 years ago is not an estate plan, it is an abandoned plan. Your needs, marital status and situations, tax bracket and health status have probably changed. If your needs have not changed, the climate of the economy has drastically changed. People get divorced and remarried, but more importantly your income, assets and health status can change in a moment's notice. Just because you "own" a plan does not mean it is an effective one. Conduct this meeting soon! I can tell you firsthand how many times people did not take my advice on this issue, and wished they had after the fact. If your house is on fire you can't call Allstate ™ and get home owner's

STEP 4

insurance as you watch it burn; you need to do it before the incident.

Action Plan (Part 1-13)

1: Elect a family member as a secretary

Instruct them to take detailed notes as each topic is discussed. You may consider video-taping the meeting as well. Many families have the "black sheep" who they do not want included at such a proceeding. Make sure that is documented as well. Just because there is a will does not mean it won't be contested by a scourged loved one. Lost sheep often come home after the death of a parent.

2: Assemble your documents

Assemble your documents; policies and contracts by type, i.e. Annuities, Life Insurance, CD's, Stocks, Bonds, and Brokerage Accounts etc. Contact each institution and verify all beneficiary designations, if applicable. Do not rely on the data contained within the policy. The beneficiary could have been changed and the contract may not have been properly updated, or the information was sent via a change of beneficiary letter, and that letter never made it inside the policy. The owner of the contract will have to call and make these requests due to privacy laws, unless your child has an in-force power-of-attorney. This is another good reason to have a properly executed power-of-attorney. In my career, I have witnessed many instances where the person who received funds after the death of a loved one was not the person who was initially designated to receive them. Be sure the beneficiary designations on all policies are current. I strongly discourage placing important documents in a safe deposit box. In the event the bank is closed when you need them it could delay your proceedings. If a document such as a life insurance policy or deed is lost, it can be replicated. A small fire proof home safe is a better way to keep your documents protected and on hand.

Charley was married at age 20 and named his mother and father as the beneficiaries on his life policy. He never changed the beneficiary on his life insurance policy after he got married. 23 years later, Charlie was killed in a car accident. His parents had preceded him in death ten years prior. Obviously, this is a problematic situation for Charlie's wife, who expected the funds from the life insurance policy.

Susan got divorced and later remarried. She never changed the beneficiary on her annuity. Upon her death, her second husband realized a little too late that the proceeds from the contract were payable to his wife's first husband. A beneficiary designation cannot be challenged in court. An insurance company is required to pay the proceeds to the last known primary beneficiary at time of death of the insured. If you have the right advisor, he/she will review your beneficiary designations on a regular basis to assure that your desires are adhered to or changed as needed. Sometimes the owner of the plan has outlived the beneficiary. Please be sure the policy has been updated with critical information such as who the new beneficiary should be. If there are second marriages, adoptions, divorces or special needs children within the family, be sure these items are addressed by a qualified elder law attorney. This may be an instance where a properly designed trust may be in order.

Find out what provisions are in place in case of a catastrophic illness. Is there a LTC policy in-force? If so, what are the benefits?

Do you have life insurance and/or annuities that have a critical illness rider? Are you currently disabled? Are you aware that some life insurance contracts have a disability waiver provision that pays all future premiums, in the event you become disabled? Many people implement these provisions at time of issue, but do

STEP 4

not realize they have the benefit available to them after they have become disabled.

Do you have long-term care insurance? Is it still in-force? If so, what are the benefits? Does it cover both nursing home and in-home care? Does it cover all levels of care that can be needed such as skilled, intermediate and custodial?

As mentioned previously, if dad was a vet who served during a time of war, he may be eligible for a benefit known as the Aid and Attendance Benefit through the Veterans Administration. According to veteranaid.org. any War-Time Veteran with 90 days of active duty, one day beginning or ending during a period of War, is eligible to apply for the Aid & Attendance Improved Pension. A surviving spouse (marriage must have ended due to death of veteran) of a War-Time Veteran may also apply. The individual applying must qualify both medically and financially. To qualify medically, a War-Time Veteran or surviving spouse must need the assistance of another person to perform daily tasks, such as eating, dressing, undressing, taking care of the needs of nature, etc. Being blind or in a nursing home for mental or physical incapacity or residing in an assisted living facility also qualifies. Eligibility must be proven by filing the proper Veterans Application for Pension or Compensation. This application will require a copy of DD-214 (To request a copy of a DD-214 visit www.vetrec.archives.gov.) or separation papers, Medical Evaluation from a physician, current medical issues, net worth limitations, and net income, along with out-of-pocket Medical Expenses. This most important benefit is overlooked by many families with Veterans or surviving spouses who need additional monies to help care for ailing parents or loved ones. This is a "Pension Benefit" and IS NOT dependent upon service-related injuries for compensation. Aid and Attendance can help pay for care in the home, Nursing Home or Assisted Living facility. A Veteran is eligible for up to $1,632 per month, while a surviving spouse is eligible for up to $1,055 per month. A couple is eligible for up to $1,949 per month*. (See website for details) If you are on a fixed income and can answer yes to these questions, then you should apply for your benefit!

According to a VA estimate, only one in seven of the widows of Vets who probably could qualify for the pension gets the monthly checks. A VA study says that the veterans generally *"are completely unaware that the program exists."* The VA knows that many veterans and widows are missing out on the benefit. Only 27 percent of veterans and 14 percent of widows receive the money. *Knight Ridder Newspapers

To qualify financially, an applicant must have on average less than $80,000 in assets, EXCLUDING their home and vehicles. If the veteran needs assistance with activities of daily living such as cooking, cleaning, or dressing, this benefit is designed to offer cash benefits in order to allow the individual to remain at home, while receiving the "aid and attendance" of another individual. Many call the VA to find they do not qualify for this benefit due to excessive assets. In some instances, the VA will allow a transfer of assets in order to allow the vet to participate in the program. Find an advisor who is well versed on this benefit and has relationships with the proper government channels and attorneys to assist.

3: Have your qualified licensed advisor perform a detailed analysis of the portfolio.

Be sure your income is enough to sustain the lifestyle you are accustomed to. If you need income, you may want to reassess the funds you have at risk once you are passed retirement age. Understanding Social Security is a very big part of this planning process. Everyone knows this government program exists, but the specifics are somewhat of an enigma to some. If you have worked during your lifetime, you and your employer(s) have paid into the Social Security system. At retirement, you receive an

STEP 4

annuity payment representing the benefits that correlate to the funds deposited. The amount received depends upon your age at inception of the benefits, your date of birth, and the type of benefits you wish to receive. All deposits are tracked via your Social Security number. If you have never explored "how much" your benefit will be when you retire, you can do so by visiting the Social Security website or calling *1-800-772-1213*.

You will receive a report showing what your benefits will be at various retirement ages, as well as what your disability and survivor's benefits would be if activated. When you are working, your Social Security tax earns credits that qualify for Social Security benefits. An employee can earn up to four credits per year based on income. Usually a beneficiary must have 40 credits or ten years of work history to be eligible for retirement benefits. Fewer credits are required for disability benefits or survivor benefits.

If you were born between 1943 and 1954, full retirement age is 66. Retirement age increases in two-month increments until age 67 for anyone who was born after 1960. Some may choose to delay their benefits in order to have an increased payment in later years. This benefit can be between six and eight percent more if delayed.

Social Security has a disability component as well if you meet the definition of disability. Once disability or retirement benefits are activated, your family members may also become eligible to benefits based on your earnings. An eligible member can be a spouse age 62 or older if married one year, a former spouse age 62 or older if you were married at least ten years, any spouse caring for a child who is under the age of 16, unmarried children under the age of 18, children who are full time students under the age of 19, or children older than 18 if disabled.

Survivor benefits exist for family members who qualify, such as a widow(er) or an ex-spouse age 60 or older (50 if disabled), widow(er) or an ex-spouse caring for a child under the age of 16 or disabled, unmarried children under age 18, children under age of 19 who are full time students through grade 12 or disabled, children older than 18 if severely disabled or your parents if they depend on your income for at least of half of their support. Your widow(er) can also receive a one-time death benefit payment of $255.

Many people do not take into consideration how they will replace the income they depend upon from two Social Security checks once one of the spouses dies. Obviously, the amount of benefits will decrease. A major component of a financial plan is where your income will come from now, and in the future, under a myriad of circumstances.

If you have not performed this type of planning, you should do so with a qualified advisor today. Your advisor can show you how much your income will be decreased when the first spouse dies. He/she can then show you ways to plan now for this event so that you are not indigent from the decrease in Social Security benefits in the future.

There are a series of myths associated with Social Security. The biggest myth is that Social Security will provide most of the income needed in retirement years. Even from inception of this entitlement, it was never intended to be an end all be all for income. In fact, the life expectancy was less than 65 years of age when the program was initiated. Many think it will be enough to live on when they quit work, but it was never intended to perform such a task. Another common myth is; you cannot earn money after you retire. This is only true of you earn money and you are collecting Social Security benefits and you are under normal retirement age. Once you are at retirement age, you can earn as much as you like. Prior to that age, $1 in benefits will be deducted for every $2, you earn above an annual limit. For 2011, that limit is $14,160. The last myth we speak of is; Social Security benefits are not taxable. Previous administrations caused a taxable event regarding Social Security benefits if you go over certain

STEP 4

thresholds. Up to 85 percent of your benefits may be taxable depending upon the amount of income you earn. A qualified advisor can show you how excess taxation may be mitigated or in some instance eliminated.

4: Is your health insurance structured properly?

Another component that is vastly over looked is health insurance after you quit working. Some people are blessed and have benefits that continue under their conventional health plan and are paid for by the former employer. In such an instance you are set! Others, however, are not so blessed. Once you reach age 65, regardless of the age you plan to quit work, Medicare becomes your primary health coverage and you will require some form of supplement. Those on Social Security are automatically enrolled. Medicare Part A is your hospital coverage. This benefit is free for all who have worked in their lifetime. There is a deductible for this benefit that generally changes every year. Part B covers physician care, laboratory tests, and physical therapy. This coverage currently has an 80/20 co-pay provision. You may purchase a Medi-Gap policy which covers the amount in excess of the part A and Part B deductible, or you may enroll in a Medicare Advantage plan. Medicare Part D refers to the prescription drug coverage for those on Medicare. You should consult a qualified advisor who can assist you in acquiring the optimum coverage that fits your needs. Plans change often as do government mandates; so, do your homework before choosing the right plan

5: Do you need "Medicaid Planning"?

As mentioned earlier, Medicaid is a program that pays medical and nursing care bills for those who are indigent. Medicaid planning means you have sheltered your countable assets, preserved assets for your loved ones, and have provided for your healthy spouse. There are two types of asset classes in Medicaid planning, countable and exempt. Countable assets are those that are made inaccessible to the state for Medicaid purposes. Countable assets and count- able income determine your Medicaid eligibility. Each state compiles this information differently so be sure you know the applicable laws which apply for your state. Usually the list includes your home, prepaid burial plots or prepaid funeral plans, term insurance and one automobile. Medicaid planning allows you to change count- able assets for exempt assets making them inaccessible to the state. Instead of paying for a nursing home bill, you can pay off the mortgage of the home, make improvements and repairs, pay off debts, purchase a car for your healthy spouse or pre-pay your burial. Do not implement any of these provisions without the advice of an elder care attorney. For those who have exhausted their long-term care benefits or have no resources to pay for the care, your benefits will come from Medicaid. Determination of benefits your state may count assets and income that are available to you for paying bills. Medicaid planning helps you create a plan to make your assets and income inaccessible. The rules and strategies are extremely complicated.

6: Once the detailed analysis is done,

Ask your advisor to perform several additional functions. The first task is a risk analysis. You may have too much of your nest egg at market risk. In periods where the market is in decline and inflation is on the rise, you may indeed outlive your money, if you cannot sustain market exposure. The second task is to prepare an income plan. Income planning is a procedure which illustrates all the vehicles that you own and how you are going to generate income at a pre- determined period. This will give you the assurance your money will not be "locked up" when you need it.

STEP 4

7: Know what you have and know how it works.

Many people "think" they have a CD from the bank and it turns out to be an annuity. That's not necessarily bad, if the annuity fits your goal structure. Others may "think" their investment is not subject to risk until the market tanks and they are in for the rude awakening to realize that they may not be able to retire when they anticipated or are forced back into the workforce just to afford their health coverage. Compile a list of all assets by class and list the benefits and drawbacks of each vehicle. Earmark each vehicle with a specific goal. By doing this you can ascertain which vehicles will be used for income, growth, rainy day fund, or simply passing on to the next generation. Now you can make educated decisions on where the money should be invested because it has a specific goal assigned.

8: Do not listen to "Aunt Millie"-

You know, the aunt who knows everything about every type of investment. "After all, her neighbor did have a reverse mortgage and lost the house, and cousin Bob put his life savings into an annuity and when the market tanked, he was broke...etc." I have witnessed many an Aunt Millie cause excess taxation, probate and even the loss of an entire portfolio because everyone listens to her "sage" advice. Just because she has been around since the Great Depression does not make her an economist. Unless she is a licensed advisor, fellowship with her, but do not heed her financial wisdom. If Aunt Millie must be present at your family meeting, be sure someone lovingly lets her know that a lot has changed in the financial world since FDR was president.

9: Real Estate

List and include primary residence, time shares, rental properties, condos, land and commercial properties. This topic will need much discussion. How much is it worth? If you do not know get it appraised. How much is owed? Are there existing liens on the property and if so, how much? How is it titled? Who gets it? Should I change the title while mom and dad are living? Answer: Get a lawyer and discuss.

10: Personal possessions

If you want that Ming vase or that special picture, tell Mom now! Don't fight over it because it was not listed in the will specifically. Be honest and open in your dialogue. Each member can make a "wish list" and you can take that information under advisement before updating or generating the will. Open discussions such as this can avoid resentment and hard feelings among your children after you have gone to be with the Lord.

11: Define the "alpha child."

If you have more than one sibling, you will need to decide who the executor or executrix of your estate shall be. It can be a shared responsibility if you "dislike" more than one of your children. (Pun intended!) The executor is the spokesperson for the family regarding settling estate matters. It is a job no one longs for. That person generally handles funeral arrangements and financial settlements as well.

12: Do you have a "do not resuscitate order" (DNR) or living will?

Where is it? Does your doctor know about its contents? Be advised that this document should be designed by a Christian attorney. There is a difference between secular and Christian views regarding this issue. Do not leave interpretations of your desires up to the state; be sure your documents are clearly written in accordance with your desires and your faith.

13: Death: We will all die.

Do you have a prepaid burial plan? Advise your children which funeral home arrangements have been made with. This would be

STEP 4

a good time to dis- cuss what type of funeral you desire: cremation or embalmment, tomb, mausoleum or grave? What type of headstone do you desire? What music would you want played at the service? What church and minister should be utilized? What garments would you like to have placed on your body? Some people don't have specific desires in this area and that is alright as well.

Pre-Paid Funeral Trust

(An option to the pre-paid funeral where you retain all control) Like most people, you've probably set aside money to pay for many of the important events in your life. Planning ahead is an important part of life if you want to make sure that you don't leave a burden for others to fix.

In the past there have been four common ways to pay for a funeral:

1. **Life Insurance**: These are funds intended to be left to your family, and may not be immediately available.
2. **Personal Savings**: These are funds for day-to-day living. In the event of a lengthy illness, they may have eroded significantly.
3. **Credit card or loan**: This approach leaves heirs with debt.
4. **Family and friends**: Borrowing from family and friends can be embarrassing, and a financial strain to repay but is often the only choice due to a lack of planning. Fortunately, there's a better option.

A funeral trust is a designated, prefunded plan that combines the financial stability of insurance with the security of a trust. Work with your licensed financial professional and establish your trust-protected final expense insurance policy easily via: A Lump sum transfer from savings, CDs, money market accounts or checking, A Transfer funds from a pre-existing life insurance account, or other unused financial investments or adding to the fund in installments over a period of years.

What happens to our "stuff" after we die? I wish I had a dollar for every person who called me after the loss of a loved one and said: "I have papers everywhere I do not know where to start." Keeping your effects in order does not have to be an arduous task. Allow me to illustrate:

When I assist clients in the death claim process generally here is what I find:

1. They have NO will or a very old, outdated will. The beneficiaries listed in the will or insurance policies are often not the people who were the intended recipients. Many people fail to update their will and beneficiary arrangements after the death of a spouse, child or after a divorce.
2. Inadequate amounts or no in-force life insurance at time of death, thus they must borrow or withdraw funds from investment contracts to pay for the funeral of a loved one.
3. The location of deeds, trusts, military papers, wills or insurance policies is unknown or in a safe deposit box.
4. Family members crawling out of the woodwork attempting to "stake a claim" on "stuff."
5. Unpaid medical or nursing care bills.
6. Estate taxes, probate and estate settlement issues.
7. Siblings and children fighting over what is left of the proceeds.

STEP 4

All these items can be and should be addressed before you take your last breath. A properly designed estate plan will rectify all the above-mentioned issues and provide a seamless transition of your estate to the intended beneficiaries upon your death.

In my line of work, I have the misfortune of talking to and counseling people about the inevitable. The most unfortunate part of my job is when you meet with a client who has just lost a loved one and in an effort to comfort you say something like, "they are in a better place now," and the response is, "I hope so." You need to be sure that you know where you will go after you leave this Earth. That can only be accomplished through a relationship with the Lord! We hope that when we take out last breath, we are in the arms of our Lord Jesus, but for some that may not happen.

The Great Commission tells us that we are to evangelize the world so that ALL will someday wit- ness the Kingdom of Heaven. As mentioned earlier, the Holy Spirit has inspired me to write this book. I feel that my "job" is first and foremost tell everyone I can about the Lord, and at that point teach them what to do with their money while they are here on Earth.

Loss of a loved one:

When your spouse or a family member dies, there is much to do. In many instances you will be forced to perform tasks that you have not done previously. It is easy to become overwhelmed with arrangements, forms, and phone calls. Some items will require immediate attention, others can wait. If you have pre-planned, it should not be as overwhelming.

Besides the financial applications regarding a funeral there is the emotional and spiritual side too. A funeral allows the family and friends of the deceased to both celebrate that person's life and mourn their death. Christian tradition has a ritual of a viewing or a wake. The ceremony is usually performed by a clergy member or friend. After the ceremony there will be legal and financial concerns that will have to be addressed. First, there is the "settlement of the estate." To settle your loved one's estate or apply for insurance proceeds or survivor's benefits, you'll need to have a number of documents. If you have properly planned, all the documents needed, will be in one accessible spot for execution by the executor named in the will. Obviously, we are assuming there "is" a will and it is updated!

Settling an estate means following legal and administrative procedures to make sure that all "debt" the estate has are paid. You may want to hire an attorney to assist you with this task. Remember these fees are part of the "probate" process we mentioned previously. Some probate expenses and taxes can be avoided, "IF", properly planning was done prior to death.

You may have to file city, state, and federal tax returns, and, if the gross estate is large enough, Form 706 (U.S. Estate Tax Return). Some states impose a state death tax or an inheritance tax; seek a qualified tax professional for advice.

If the deceased had an in-force life insurance contract(s), a death claim must be filed with each carrier. An original death certificate must accompany each death claim.

If you have more than one policy with the same carrier, generally, only one death certificate will be required. Be sure to order an adequate number of death certificates from the funeral director. There will be instances in the future when you will need to produce a death certificate even after you have settled the estate. Contact your spouse or ex-spouse's employer as well as the Social Security Administration (SSA) to see if you are eligible to file a claim for survivor's or death benefits. Make your plan now, so your family is taken care of when you pass. Putting this off only hurts those you have worked too hard to protect!

STEP 4

Life Insurance

Shaniqua and Tyrone were not prepared for the horrific curve life had thrown them. Their daughter Sylvia had passed away suddenly after an illness, leaving behind a two- year-old child. Sylvia was unmarried and did not have life insurance. Her parents were forced to acquire the funds for her burial from funds previously set aside for retirement. Shaniqua and Tyrone are also faced with the task of raising their granddaughter. If Sylvia had adequate life insurance at the time of her premature demise, her parents could have paid for the burial, possessed the resources to raise their granddaughter and possibly funded her college.

As the Bible states, we do not know when we will be called home. I encourage everyone who reads this book to have a review of your existing life insurance coverage done right away. You cannot afford to be without this coverage.

To many, life insurance is viewed as a policy you buy from a guy who drives a Cadillac and wears a cheap polyester suit. Now that you have that picture burned into your brain, let me dispel the myths associated with life insurance. I have had thousands of people tell me they don't need it, don't believe in it, or can't afford it. I have NEVER had a widow or widower say no thanks when they got their check.

Depending upon your age, marital and family status, and job description, every- one's life insurance needs will be different. If you have just started a family, you need coverage for catastrophic events such as paying off the home or providing your children with an education after you have passed. If you are in retirement years, life insurance becomes the perfect vehicle for transferring money to the next generation and paying for estate taxes and settlement costs. Allow me to explain.

If you are not in retirement years and have a need for a large death benefit, but do not have the resources to pay for the coverage. Term coverage is very inexpensive and may be the way for you to go. You can acquire a large death benefit with a low annual premium utilizing term coverage.

This is perfect for a young family just starting out who may have small children to provide for in the event they pass away at a young age. It is also applicable in many business applications for buy/sell agreements etc. I encourage term insurance for these applications. There are many quality insurance companies to choose from. Check the company's ratings before you buy.

Buying term and invest the difference was a popular saying in the past, does it still hold true today? I say no. With the recent market turmoil many have lost what they have been saving. Will the market come back? Maybe, I do not know. I am not an analyst. I can tell you however, that for those who purchased a permanent life insurance policy such as whole life contracts have some cash value in those contracts. In some instances that cash value in those policies may supersede the value of some stock portfolios. If you were saving the difference and that money was lost, you are farther behind than if you purchased a contract that accumulated cash value. Every situation is different and careful attention must be given to your goals and desires before implementing a program, but you must look at all possible scenarios when implementing such a plan. Be sure you are aware of all variables. So once again, this advice is strongly predicated upon who you choose to deal with for your estate planning needs.

Many people have opinions different than mine, but the numbers do not lie. Be careful of an advisor or insurance agent who proposes the cancelation of an existing whole life or universal life policy in order to pitch a term policy. While buying term and investing the difference works on paper, no one really does it. They end up with an expensive term policy that self- destructs in the future when they are much older and cannot afford the increase in premium to keep the coverage in force.

STEP 4

Life Insurance has always been the vehicle of choice for those in an estate tax crisis. Obviously, the parameters change on those who are in a "crisis" depending upon where the "sun sets" on the federal estate tax exemption amount and top tax bracket. This is commonly called the Bush tax cuts. Many high net worth clients are looking to life insurance as the product that will rescue their ill-liquid assets, that may have lost most of its value in the recent market doldrums.

Every estate planning relies upon two things: market performance and longevity. Life insurance eliminates both risks, while providing the means to replenish one's resources. Life insurance can also secure a retirement income stream while preserving assets for the next generation.

Donald A. Galade

Enclosed is a list of items you should discuss with your advisor and attorney:

- Loss of a Spouse/Family Member
- Planning/Paying for a Funeral
- Organizing Your Finances after Your Spouse Has Died
- Developing a Spending Plan
- Credit Reports (what's on it)
- Life Insurance: Protection Planning and beneficiary designations
- Claiming Life Insurance Benefits
- Health Coverage: Overview
- Long-Term Care Insurance (LTCI)
- Inheriting an IRA or Employer-Sponsored Retirement Plan
- Claiming Survivor's and Death Benefits
- Social Security Survivor's Benefits and the Lump-Sum Death Benefit
- Military Benefits
- Settling an Estate
- Filing a Final Income Tax Return
- Income in Respect of a Decedent
- Filing an Estate Tax Return
- Table of Estate Tax Brackets and Exemption Limits
- Steps to Estate Planning Success
- Social Security Survivor's Benefits
- Investment Planning—The Basics
- Retirement Planning—The Basics
- Estate Planning—An Introduction
- Gift and Estate Taxes
- Choosing an Income Tax Filing Status
- Wills/Trust

STEP 4

Action Plan (Part 14-17)

14: Wills, trusts, power-of-attorney documents

Do they exist? How old are they? Has any- thing changed in your life since they were created? Do you have an attorney who is a specialist in elder law? If you do not have one, find one soon. Be sure they are specifically an elder law attorney. Any attorney can generate a will, but only those who specialize in elder law know the constantly changing laws that affect trusts, P.O.A.'s, and Medicare/Medicaid nursing care rules.

15: Maintenance

Once you have completed steps 1-12, the experts you have chosen to assemble an estate plan. Be sure to review the plan at least once a year with the same professionals and address any changes that have taken place in your life since the last time you met. Do not shop for these professionals based on price. You should know how they are compensated and have transparency in your dealings, but do not base your decision to hire a professional based on their fee schedule. Many people put more thought and money into their "last vacation" then they do their estate plan. It's this small-minded thinking that gives the Aunt Millie's of the world all their pearls of wisdom. You spent a lifetime creating an estate and it can be gone in a heartbeat because of few bad choices. Pray about the advisors and attorneys you need in your life, and God will place them in your path. If you have the best people on the case, your chances of succeeding are greatly improved.

16: Protecting against identity theft

Identity theft is one of the fastest growing crimes in our generation. New schemes are being invented by thieves daily. Many thinks losing a wallet or purse is just about cancelling the credit cards. That is the least of the worries you have. Today's criminals know that you are going to stop the cards accessibility as soon as it is stolen. What they want is your personal information. They will use that information to generate a new identity and pretend they are you. This new identity will bring a world of hurt into your life. Knowing how to protect yourself is important. Knowing what to do if you become a victim is crucial.

Check your credit report at least once a year to be sure there is no suspicious activity. Visit www.annualcreditreport.com or call *1-877-322-8228.*

Note: www.annualcreditreport.com *is the site you want to visit for your free annual credit reports. Other sites boast they will provide such information, but in order to acquire the reports you may have to subscribe to one of the credit reporting repairing services that company offers. Also note there are many who boast they can fix your credit. If you have delinquencies on that report that are truly caused by late payments, the only way to fix such delinquencies is to pay the debt. Granted, if there are items on your report that are not yours or are wrongly reported then this is something that can be rectified.*

Do not carry your check book, all your credit cards and other charge cards with you at the same time. In many instances you will not need to have all that credit potential with you all at once. Take only what you will need. Keep receipts of everything you purchase. Do not leave potential credit information or remnants of the same around for others to view. Save your receipts and check them against your statements when you receive them. Shred all paper, period. Be careful when you use an ATM so that no one can see your hand on the activation pad and acquire your PIN. Do not give personal information to anyone on the phone, ever. If a legitimate creditor wishes to discuss your account, they should have the data needed to do so. Do not give out dates of birth, Social Security numbers, driver's license numbers and especially account numbers to anyone, ever. Period! Do not keep Social Security cards in your wallet or purse. Memorize the number and keep it locked away in a safe place at home. Never have your number pre-printed on checks or any other documents. Keep special care to any document that you must transport such as an income tax form that may have your number printed on it. In the event the document is lost or taken from you, the thief can become YOU within hours.

If you are a victim of ID theft call all major credit reporting agencies at once and report the theft.

- Equifax: www.equifax.com *800-685-1111*
- Experian: www.experian.com *888-397-3742*
- Transunion: www.transunion.com *800-916-8800*
- Stop telemarketing calls by calling *888-382-1222* or registering online at www.donotcall.gov
- Remove your name from email and mailing lists by visiting https://dmachoice.thedma.org/ and www.optoutprescreen.com.

When you get rid of a computer, be sure to remove the hard drive and destroy it separately from the computer. I suggest soaking it in a bucket of water then to be sure dismantle it.

Discarded computers are the biggest resource of identity information and Social Security information to an ID thief. Only open legitimate emails and be sure to install proper spyware, malware, virus protection and internet security software on your computer. Also know what sites your children are always visiting and monitor their computer usage by keeping the PC In a common area.

17: Windfall

If you follow the precepts of this book, I pray that you would receive a financial windfall. In such a case there are some things you should be aware of in order to stay in God's will and do the right thing with your resources. First, be sure you have the proper team of advisors, attorneys, CPA's, and insurance professionals to be sure you acquire the right advice. Ascertain the best use of the windfall. You may want to pay off debt, save for a rainy day, fund a child's education fund, or retirement. Remember that *"to whom much is given, much is required"**, and be sure to replenish the storehouse from which you are fed with 10 percent of the windfall. Then set up a plan to invest for the future. Prepare an estate plan for what will become of your assets after your demise.

*Luke 12:48, King James Version

STEP 5:

How to Find the Right Advisor

Many advisors talk about strategies, or how to re-allocate a portfolio. Asset allocation is the real key to sustained growth in a portfolio, not market timing. You cannot manage your portfolio based on short term gains and losses, but long-term results as it correlates to the assigned goal of the funds.

My income is derived by helping people plan. Whether it is income planning, tax planning, estate planning or retirement planning, our firm assists a client with identifying their financial goals and developing a strategy, or blueprint, to achieve them. So, as you can guess, the question I get asked the most is: "what should I invest in?" This is not an easy question to answer. We spend a great deal of time with our clients acquiring information in order to prepare a comprehensive analysis before we can address the question of where to place a client's funds. A great deal of information must be obtained before a recommendation can be made. I liken my practice to that of a doctor.

When you go to a new practitioner for the first time, he/she must obtain your family history and medical information. The doctor must know what you are allergic too, or where it hurts before they can prescribe a course of treatment. The same is true with your investment strategy. You can prepare a forensically designed financial plan based on your risk tolerance, tax bracket, desired income level and goal structure, or you can take the advice of every stock broker that comes along with the latest tip on how to "bag the elephant." Take my advice; find an advisor that will build a platform in which your portfolio sits, rather than throwing darts at the Wall Street Journal in the hopes of timing the next bull market.

If you have a specific need, find a professional that is an expert in that field and utilize them. Stop purchasing stocks on "tips" and buying funds or bank products without a clear and concise goal as what it is you expect these funds to do for you. Using the right advisor is the key to a successful strategy. If you used a "salesman" who just offers products, you will ultimately get burned. Utilize a professional who knows the laws and regulations on all matters of estate planning and investing.

When you are young you can go to the general practitioner for all your medical needs. As you mature, it is the specialists that keep you alive and well. As you get older, you notice that it is the "specialists" that you visit most. Your family doctor recommends you see the heart specialist not because the family doctor doesn't know how to treat you; but since the specialist is the expert in this field. Do not use a general practitioner with your retirement money and estate planning needs.

When you are young you have the luxury of time on your side. As you get older and face the inherent threat of outliving your money or losing it with one long-term illness, you need a specialist. You need someone who knows the laws, regulations and caveats that affect folks in retirement years. Do not trust the crucial decisions you must make in your golden years to a general practitioner, and please do not "shop for price" to get the "best deal" on your planning needs. This is not a used car; it's your entire life's savings. The on-line site that you use to generate a will may be fine for some but beware it does not come with an online lawyer to defend it when something is challenged after you

STEP 5

die. Seek out the best licensed, knowledgeable, Christian advisor(s) and attorneys in your area and utilize them.

Not all advisors are the same. Many choose products for a client that may be more in line with the advisors' best interests than that of the client. Some advisors sell the same products or services to all their clients. One cannot say a product is either good or bad for every person. So, before you sign up with an advisor, do some homework. Have a list of questions and concerns ready for the professional you are thinking about utilizing and interview them.

It is especially helpful if you can find an advisor an attorney and an accountant who have a good working relationship with each other. We live in a litigious society. I have seen families break up over $5,000 let alone $5,000,000. It does not matter what size your estate is, you need a plan, and a Christian plan. You can make many decisions regarding your finances and your "stuff," without getting God involved, but I would not recommend it. If your estate planner or financial advisor notices you will have an estate tax issue upon your death, this is a great time to fix that by giving some money to God, while you are alive. Now I am not on the payroll at any church, nor am I directly related to any "annual appeal," but since you can't take it with you, and Uncle Sam may get a share bigger than he deserves, why not solve both problems by sending it on ahead of you. A Christian advisor can assist. If you do not have one, pray about it and then find one! There are websites that can assist you in locating the right individual for your needs.

To find a qualified advisor you need to ask specific questions about his/her practice. You need to be sure you are getting good advice. You would not seek the services of a plumber if you needed surgery. Be sure to match the services you need with the provider you are using. Even if you have a qualified advisor currently, a second opinion from a Christian business professional will either confirm or deny your decision to use the professional you have chosen. If a doctor told you surgery was needed, you would seek a second opinion. Why then would you not seek a second opinion on your second biggest asset, your nest egg? Be sure you are not paying taxes on funds you do not need. Be sure your money will last the test of time. Question if a ROTH conversion is in your best interest at this time but be sure an alternative minimum tax (AMT) is not triggered in the process.

Enclosed you will find just a few of the many questions that are considered industry standard. You can find a wonderfully detailed questionnaire for auditioning advisors on John Hancock's web site. I invite you to visit this site for a much more extensive list.

Experience:

- What is your educational background?
- What is your experience and how long have you been in the industry?
- What are your credentials?
- Do you have a specialty?
- What licenses do you currently have?
- Do you carry errors and omissions insurance and what amount?
- Can you provide references?

Payment:

- How are your fees or commissions paid, and what are they?
- Do you have a minimum fee or minimum account balance requirement?
- All financial professionals make money by offering products. You need to know how the individual you are working with gets paid.

STEP 5

Services Provided:
- How many clients do have?
- Will you provide a detailed written financial plan including your recommendations?

Be leery of advisors who make claims that are too good to be true and cannot back up what they are saying with statistics and evidence. Also, if the person you are working with is suggesting excessive trades or policy conversions and they do not do a comprehensive fact find to ascertain your investment goals and objectives first, you may want to find another advisor. The most important facet of an estate plan is the information shared with your advisor. Your estate planning professional should gather a multitude of facts about your current and expected financial situations before any recommendations could be entertained. Enclosed is a sample of an estate planning fact finding document I utilize in my practice. Your advisor should utilize something like this or at least contain the same amount of information in order to do a proper review of your financial health. This is yet another advantage in dealing with a professional who is equally yoked with you on a spiritual level.

With the recent stock market debacle and current turbulent economy, I spend more time teaching people how to keep their assets rather than earn interest on them. Some are happy to get a return of their money let alone a return on it. I find solace in the Word for everything in life, especially our finances. I find that advisors who do not do a thorough job with asset allocation for the client generally based the allocations on the advisor's needs rather than that of the client. Remember the market goes up and down, if you lost money, it is not the markets fault. You may be working with an advisor who has not done his/her homework properly on your behalf. Income may be more important than growth. Although both are crucial, without proper income planning, you will be forced to spend down principal thus "out-live" your money. Before you decide what is allocated to savings and investments you must ascertain what your current and future income needs will be. Enclosed is a simple income calculator that can help you access your income needs.

You should have a complete inventory of your entire value of your estate. A sample inventory check list can be found on-line. Documenting all personal, financial and historical stat for future generations will not only help establish your estate plan but also serve as a guide creating your legacy plan.

STEP 5

Good Record Keeping

Below is a sample of pertinent information that should be recorded and kept with your will and other important documents.

- **Name**
- **Social Security Number**
- **Employer:** Name, Address, Phone
- **Doctor:** Name, Address, Phone
- **Lawyer:** Name, Address, Phone
- **Accountant:** Name, Address, Phone
- **Minister:** Name, Address, Phone
- **Safe Deposit Box:** Bank, Address, Phone
- **Certificate of Deposit:** Bank, Address, Phone, Account Number
- **Checkbook:** Bank, Address, Phone, Account Number
- **Savings Passbook:** Bank, Address, Phone, Accounts
- **Money Market Accounts:** Bank, Address, Phone, Accounts
- **Stock Certificates:** Account Number, Institution, Address, Phone
- **Security Records:** Account Number, Institution, Address, Phone
- **Life Insurance**:
    - Company
    - Policy Number
    - Beneficiaries
    - Annuities
    - Funeral Home Preference
    - Deposition of Remains
    - Cemetery Preference
    - Prepaid Expenses (Yes/No)
        - Attach receipts of prepaid funeral expenses to this document including any special requests.

BONUS:
The Long-Term Effects

The data compiled for this chapter has been derived from several sources, used with permission. I document the source, and in some instances re-produce the data in its entirety to show that the advice, and or opinions are that of other industry experts and not my own opinion. This is done to educate my readers on basic economic theories. There will always be opposing points of view. Your task is to gather data and use your own discernment.

One of the contributing factors to the fall of the economy was what is referred to as the mortgage crisis. People purchased houses they simply could not afford, largely in part because the government relaxed the lending qualifications, and greedy mortgage brokers gave loans to people who should not have borrowed in the first place. I did not say the people should not have received a loan; however, they should not have received a loan for a house they could not afford. There are very specific guidelines as to how much debt you can have predicated upon your income and past credit history. There is a very good reason for this is it just works. If I make $1,000 a week, I cannot afford a mortgage payment of $3,000 a month. The numbers simply do not work. With a period of very low interest rates over the past several years, many people purchased homes with what is known as an adjustable interest rate. The rate can go up or down depending upon the climate set by the Fed. Say you purchased a $250,000 house and had a mortgage payment of $1500. The payment was predicated on an initial adjustable interest rate of five percent. When the climate changes and interest rates go up, your mortgage payment escalates as well. You now have a house you cannot afford, where previously it was affordable.

The loans were then bundled together and sold by organizations like Fannie Mae and Freddie Mac to other institutional investment firms. These institutions created mutual funds based on the parameters of the loans. Many of these mortgage-backed securities ended up in your retirement portfolio and 401(k) plan. As people could no longer afford the mortgage payment on their homes, they simply walked away from the properties, and let the bank foreclose. If the bank was stuck with the property, it obviously was not receiving the mortgage payment, thus the loan went into default. If the loan went into default, the investment which was backed by the loan within a mutual fund or a security product was worthless. Since a portion of your investable assets were made up of worth- less debt, your 401(k) became a 201(k) (pun intended).

Wall Street reacted accordingly. The market tumbled, which caused spiraling job losses and a failing economy. Big Brother reacted and thought printing more money (thus going further in debt) would spur the economy, but the situation got worse.

It all started with the government relaxing the rules, so they could look like heroes to those who would not normally be able to buy a home. Greed fueled the lending industry to be at the right place at the right time.

So, those who can afford their homes may witness the collateral damage (pun intended) from this and possibly lose their jobs. Now they, too, may have to worry about their home because they can no longer afford the payments. "I'm from the government, I am here to help!"

We cannot dismiss the importance of discussing the future impact of Obama-Care and other recent governmental initiatives as they relate to where our country is headed financially. Government spending, TARP, cap and tax, the stimulus package, and recession are topics in the headlines regularly, but does the average person really understand the fleecing America is getting?

The shrapnel grenade our government has thrown at us will have a ripple effect for generations to come, and no one is aware of the true consequences. We have buried our heads in the sand so long we may never recover. Income, capital gains and estate taxes will inevitably, increase. Medicare, Medicaid and other entitlement programs will witness drastic cuts. This means more out of pocket costs for those on a fixed income.

It will not be long before we see a dramatic impact on our economy as the true long- term effects of our government spending are realized by the rest of the world. The strength of the dollar as it relates to the Euro or the Yen plays a major role in the global economy.

Europe is witnessing the long-term effects of overspending. Greece is insolvent, Portugal has a liquidity problem, Belgium, France and even the UK have financial issues, and Russia may be the next to fall (again).

World leaders seem to think they can keep the status quo and in the words of the infamous Bob Marley, *"everything is gonna be alright."* Well, the financial landscape of the world is anything but *"Irie Mon!"*

This vast debt could trigger a recession unlike anything we have ever seen. Congress is frantically trying to increase the debt ceiling to prevent the U.S from defaulting on debt payments for the first time in history. How ironic, isn't this the same thing that sparked the economic collapse to begin with? "Don't worry; I'm from the government I'm here to help."

BONUS

According to an Associated Press-GFK poll, 41 percent oppose this idea and 38 percent are in favor. Don't you love these polls? Why do they never add up to 100 percent? Do you think it takes 21 percent of the populous to administer the poll, so their votes don't count? It's probably just that 78 percent of all statistics are made up on the spot, just like this one. You can watch four different broadcasts and get four different opinions on where we are going. Here's a revelation: it ain't good!

> *"It is not, perhaps, unreasonable to conclude, that a pure and perfect democracy is a thing not attainable by man, constituted as he is of contending elements of vice and virtue, and ever mainly influenced by the predominant principle of self-interest. It may, indeed, be confidently asserted, that there never was that government called a republic, which was not ultimately ruled by a single will, and, therefore, (however bold may seem the paradox,) virtually and substantially a monarchy."*

-Alexander Fraser Tytler http://www.iwise.com/

It is obvious that the stimulus package has done little to create jobs or spur the economy. Government does not create jobs; people create jobs by starting new small businesses. Wall Street, big banks and the major unions witnessed a windfall from the Fed using our tax dollars. Little was done to stimulate the current economic situation by means of funding small businesses which are the backbone of our country's workforce.

Donald A. Galade

The Ultimate Outcome:

Economists say unprecedented taxation will soon be imposed as we begin to see the kind of inflation financial analysts have been promising since the financial meltdown began in 2007. Put the two together – soaring inflation and higher taxes – and we get the rest of a real witches' brew. To call Wall Street "unsettled" in this upcoming environment is an understatement...

The role of the government will continue to grow in the single largest sector of the US economy: health care. The poor will get additional new subsidies. The upper-middle income wage earner now considered "wealthy," will pay more and more taxes. Reduced insurance company subsidies might force carriers to leave the health care business, thus reducing the pool of competition. Smaller subsidies for hospitals and nursing homes will eventually lead to rising prices, with nursing homes becoming "selective" in alarming new ways – like disqualifying people on government programs in favor of those with more expensive long-term care insurance.

By sheer necessity and for the survival of our nation, a new law will eventually be enacted to eradicate debt and balance the budget, but it may take decades. Until then, retirees have a lot more to worry about than waiting for a solvent economy. As the effect of debt and deficit escalate, we can probably expect a series of traumatic market corrections to destabilize a struggling national economy.

(Original Informational sources for attribution: Landmark: The Inside Story of America's New Health Care Law and What It Means for Us All by the Washington Post Staff; AARP Bulletin, Special Section: Unser's Guide to Health Care Reform, May 2010, by Patricia Barry; Decoding Generational Differences/The Private Client Reserve, US Bank, by Colby Johnson)

America was once the largest producer of goods and services in the world. Our economy flourished after WWII as we became a world leader for exporting goods abroad. That is no longer the case.

BONUS

"The North American Free Trade Agreement or NAFTA is an agreement signed by the governments of Canada, Mexico, and the United States, creating a trilateral trade bloc in North America. The agreement came into force on January 1, 1994. NAFTA's effects, both positive and negative, have been quantified by several economists, whose findings have been reported in publications such as the World Bank's Lessons from NAFTA for Latin America and the Caribbean, NAFTA's Impact on North America, and NAFTA Revisited by the Institute for International Economics. Some argue that NAFTA has been positive for Mexico, which has seen its poverty rates fall and real income rise (in the form of lower prices, especially food), even after accounting for the 1994–1995 economic crisis. Others argue that NAFTA has been beneficial to business owners and elites in all three countries but has had negative impacts on farmers in Mexico who saw food prices fall based on cheap imports from U.S. agribusiness, and negative impacts on U.S. workers in manufacturing and assembly industries who lost jobs. Critics also argue that NAFTA has contributed to the rising levels of inequality in both the U.S. and Mexico. Some economists believe that NAFTA has not been enough (or worked fast enough) to produce an economic convergence, nor to substantially reduce poverty rates. Some have suggested that in order to fully benefit from the agreement, Mexico must invest more in education and promote innovation in infrastructure and agriculture."

Source: https://en.wikipedia.org/wiki/Nafta

Most of the manufacturing of goods has since departed America and has taken up root in Mexico and China. We are now a country which consumes more than we pro- duce. Many of the manufacturing companies have moved to foreign soil for the benefits of cheaper labor and far fewer governmental regulations and compliance. Imagine that! Thus, we regulated ourselves out of a job, literally, and then blame the illegals. Many of these companies have former employees who still collect pension plans. People were not expected to live if they do today when these pension plans were created. Many of the company's earnings must be allocated to fund previously implemented pension plans. In order to remain competitive in the world market, many companies had "no choice" but to pull up stakes and relocate on foreign shores. Granted, NAFTA may have made these decisions easier. Since the economies of China and Mexico have witnessed an explosion from the products they export to the U.S., the exchange rate between the dollar and the yen for example, are watched very closely by the entire world. Thus, the creation of the G20 Summit or group of 20 as it is called. The G20 was established in 1999, in the wake of the 1997 Asian Financial Crisis, to bring together major advanced and emerging economies to stabilize the global financial market. Did you get that? Since its inception, the G20 has held annual Finance Ministers and Central Bank Governors' Meetings and dis- cussed measures to promote the financial stability of the world and to achieve a sustain- able economic growth and development.

Source: http://www.g20.org

Portfolio Status

Did Your Portfolio "Recover?" Do You Feel "Stimulated?" Some Don't.

The 21st century has certainly gotten off to a rocky start. First, there was the collapse of the Tech Bubble. The Fed tells us that from 2000 to 2002 U.S. households lost $6.5 trillion in value from their portfolios, pensions, and 401(k)s. A mere six years later, the Housing Bust of 2008 more than doubled the damage, coming in at a whopping $15.5 trillion dollars in lost value!

Obviously, our economy is in a tumultuous time. To say we have a turbulent economy is a bit of an understatement. The greatest economic minds of our generation are guessing as to what strategies to use to prevent economic collapse. Unprecedented government spending and deficits are clouding our future. Industry terms like "flash crash" are created daily to explain situations that occur within the market. Some analysts predict a rally while others tell of the impending doom of our entire economy. As an advisor, I can see some validity in both previously mentioned points of view; as a Christian, I can tell you the Bible speaks of financial turmoil in the end times.

In the first 185 years of our nation's history where financial records were maintained (i.e., the period from 1789-1974), the USA spent $3.8 trillion in aggregate.

The total of projected government outlays during the current 2010 fiscal year is $3.7 trillion.

Source: Office of Management and Budget.

On March 2, 2005, then Fed Chairman Alan Greenspan told the House Budget

Committee that the US government needed to undertake *"major deficit-reducing actions."* Greenspan said, *"I fear we may have already committed more physical resources to the baby-boom generation in its retirement years than our economy has the capacity to deliver".*

Source: House of Representatives.

Prior to 1971, the dollar was represented by a fixed amount of gold. The government guaranteed this convertibility and it could not just "print" money at will. Post-1971, the U.S. went off the gold standard there by, lifting the restrictions on how much money could be printed. To complicate this, there is more money in existence currently than there is gold in existence, one of the governments's biggest factors in removing the gold standard in the first place. These actions devalue the dollar which can cause a global economic crisis, since the dollar is a benchmark against many foreign currencies.

As of November 2010, gold has reached an all-time high cresting $1,422. Robert B. Zoellick, the president of the World Bank, announced that the world should be placed back on the "gold system." Gold is the "elephant in the room" that must be addressed by policymakers, as it's being used as an alternative monetary asset because of unease about the strength of developed economies, Robert Zoellick, president of the World Bank, was quoted by CNBC. The response by the conservative right was quick. *"We don't want temporary, artificial economic growth brought at the expense of permanently higher inflation which will erode the value of our incomes and our savings,"* retorted Sarah Palin, the former GOP Vice Presidential nominee. *"We want a stable dollar combined with real economic reform. It's the only way we can get our economy back on the right track,"* she said."

A gold standard simply will not work! There is not enough gold in the world to support the amount of currency in circulation. That is why the floating exchange system was implemented back in 1971. From that time till now, obviously the amount of currency in use has gone up substantially. Mr. Zoellick's point was to illustrate the fact that our monetary system is broken.

If the dollar is worth less, it is only a matter of time until it is worthless. Obviously, the buying power will continue to diminish. When the buying power is less, inflation rates escalate. Although inflation is a normal component in a balanced economy, it is my professional opinion that we will enter a period of hyper-inflation soon. It could come to the point where your currency may have more value as a literal fuel for heat than it does as a purchasing agent for goods and services.

The devaluing of the American dollar is no accident. It has been the intention of the Federal Reserve for many years. Before I can develop this topic, you must first fully understand who and what the Federal Reserve is. First, The Federal Reserve is an oxymoron. The institution is not controlled by the federal government and there is no reserve. It was Alexander Hamilton who lobbied for the first private Federal Bank, and in 1789 Congress chartered the bank.

> *"I place economy among the first and most important virtues, and public debt as the greatest of dangers. To preserve our independence, we must not let our rulers load us with perpetual debt."*

-Thomas Jefferson

Thomas Jefferson was adamantly opposed to the idea of a privately-owned federal bank and said, *"I sincerely believe the banking institutions having the issuing power of money are more dangerous to liberty than standing armies."* In 1811, under President James Madison, Vice President George Clinton broke the tie vote in Congress to cast the bankers out refusing to renew their charter. Unfortunately, it was President Madison who proposed a second United States privately owned Central Bank, and it came into existence 1816. When speaking to his closest friend, Martin Van Buren, Andrew Jackson said, *"The bank, is trying to kill me, but I will kill it!"* (And he did) The year is now 1913, the year after Woodrow Wilson was elected president of the United States. Prior to his election he needed financial support to pay for his campaign, so he reluctantly agreed, that, if elected, he would sign the Federal Reserve Act in return for that financial support. In December 1913, while many members of Congress were home for Christmas, the Federal Reserve Act was rammed through Congress and was later signed by President Wilson. Later, Wilson admitted with remorse, when referring to the Fed. *"I have unwittingly ruined my country."*

We didn't have, nor did we need, an income tax until we got the bankers back. The income tax was only needed to pay interest to the bankers for our money that they loaned to our government. Yes, you read that right, the Fed, mostly on paper, creates money or pays the Treasury a small printing fee for currency, and then lends this money to our government. Our taxes pay them interest on this loan that costs the FED virtually nothing to make. What a sweetheart of a deal they have.

"One of the most ungodly and fraudulent institutions ever perpetrated on the American people and the world, is the Federal Reserve System which through deceit became the central bank of the United States in 1913. The idea came about on a meeting in Jekyll Island off the coast of Georgia in 1910. The bankers in this country, especially J.P. Morgan, created a currency panic in 1907 in order to get the American people to accept the idea of a central bank."

A central bank already existed in England from as far back as 1694. The Rothschild's completely dominate the banking system. It is estimated their wealth goes into the trillions.

Baron Nathan Mayer Rothschild boasted: *"I care not what puppet is placed upon the throne of England to rule the Empire on which the sun never sets. The man that controls Britain's money supply controls the British Empire, and I control the British money supply."* The idea of a central bank is to so enslave the people of the country to a debt money system that you continue to collect taxes continuously which just covers the interest. The duped people of the United States are paying about $400 billion dollars per year to the IRS which is the collection agency for the Federal Reserve. By the way, the Federal Reserve is a privately-owned bank with 10 private members. The Chase Manhattan

Bank is a member which is owned by the Rockefellers who are Rothschild Agents. At this point the citizens of the United States falsely owe these lemmings over 10 trillion dollars. Have you ever asked the following question? WHO HAS THAT MUCH MONEY TO LOAN TO THE UNITED STATES? Now that the Federal Reserve was firmly in place, schemes had to be constructed to get the government to borrow so a continuously growing national debt would happen. So here are some coincidences: The Federal Reserve is created in 1913, and then in 1914 we have World War 1. Right at the end of World War 1, we have a depressed economy especially in the Weimar Republic where 2 billion marks could buy a loaf of bread. In 1917, we had the Bolshevik revolution in Russia. A man named Lord Alfred Milner was a front man and paymaster for the Rothschild's in Petrograd during the revolution. He later headed a secret organization called The Round Table which was dedicated to a one world government run by wealthy financiers under socialism.

Then, lo and behold, in the 1920's we see a little-known corporal with 12 men meeting in a beer hall in Munich while in America the Roaring 20's were in progress until October,

1929. Then the Federal Reserve withheld money from circulation, so bills could not be paid, while simultaneously they were calling in all their loans which caused the stock market to crash. By 1932 the price of stocks had plummeted 80 percent. When the bankers plunged this nation into a depression on that fateful day in October, at the New York Stock Exchange was a visitor, his name was Winston Churchill who stated after the crash of '29, *"Now I know who wields the real power."* The key to understanding the Great Depression is to realize that when the Federal Reserve had contracted the money supply, there was not enough money in circulation to pay bills, to hire people, to pay back loans, etc. The crash of the stock market was the symptom, but the cause was the Fed restricting the money supply. This is their weapon which is used today. When they flood the country with money, this causes inflation.

For more detailed information on the Federal Reserve, please read: "The Creatures from Jekyll Island" by G. Edward Griffin.

"Let's print 'till we run out'a paper and if we run out'a paper we'll borrow some from China!"

Federal Reserve Chairman Ben Bernanke said he wouldn't monetize the US debt but later he recanted on his word and approved the printing of $600 billion. The goal is to pump money into the economy in order to purposely devalue the dollar and sends prices for goods and services skyrocketing. The dust had not quit settled on the midterm election of 2010 when the FED made the announcement. Since the days of bail outs, tarp and stimulus are gone forever via the new conservative regime change, the FED figured they would have to take things into their own hands to move they're along the agency that is already in place. Because they are as we said, un-audited and unregulated they can do what they want, when they want, thus they have the future of our economy in their hands. These goals can be accomplished outside the realm of government control by the nature of the FED's existence.

As the FED monetizes the national debt to "inflate it away" other countries try to protect their currency. We now face a new "currency war." The Federal Reserve began purchasing US Treasury notes and bonds with the principal income it receives from its vast holdings of Fannie Mae and Freddie Mac mortgage securities. This practice wherein the Fed buys up US government securities and injects cash into the public market as payment for these securities - is a form of monetizing the debt.

The last time the Fed did this on a big scale was back in the 1960's when it attempted to mop up the excess treasury securities that were flooding the market as a result of Lyndon Johnson's efforts to finance the Vietnam War. That Fed program was viewed at the time as a failure, since the cash the Fed put back into the economy in exchange for the securities was a big reason - perhaps the major reason - why price inflation accelerated from the late 1960's.

The market was expecting some sort of monetary stimulus, but not this. The expectation was that the Fed would renew its "quantitative easing" program involving Fannie Mae and Freddie Mac securities - a program designed to push down long-term mortgage rates. That program was successful inasmuch as mortgage rates are at record lows, but it left the Fed with well over a trillion dollars of these securities on its balance sheet. Fed officials have lately been pondering publicly how to get rid of these securities, and apparently have concluded they can't under present market conditions without forcing mortgage rates back up again, which would only hurt the housing market. Instead, these officials have concluded that the Fed has no choice but to hold on to these securities until they mature, which is well over 10 years from now for the portfolio. The Fed receives billions of dollars of principal and interest payments every year on this portfolio, and what to do with this cash has always been open for discussion until now. But using principal proceeds from these securities to monetize the government debt is fraught with risk. For one, should the housing market start to weaken again, and foreclosures rise from current levels, the Fed will be sitting on billions of dollars of credit losses on its portfolio. This could eat up most if not all the profit it would otherwise earn on this portfolio. Second, older investors have memories of the nasty inflationary consequences the last time the Fed monetized the debt, and the market has become very skittish about the risk of inflation, and maybe even hyperinflation Weimar Germany, that could result from the enormous fiscal and monetary stimulus put into the economy since 2007.

Donald A. Galade

Source: http://www.thepeoplesvoice.org/TPV3/index.php

Every generation has the desire to see their children become more successful than the previous. Until recently this was the norm. Now I believe it will be the exception. The children of today will be the first generation of Americans that will not have more opportunity than their parents. In a recent article published by protect seniors. org, a former Federal Reserve Bank Chairman had stated:

The vast majority of American retirees see their children and grandchildren being unable to participate in the "American Dream" and afford retirement. According to a poll conducted by protectseniors.org, in conjunction with former White House ERISA advisor, Dr. Thomas Mackell Jr., Ph.D., almost three quarters of poll participants said that they expect their children and grandchildren to have worse career and lifestyle opportunities than they enjoyed (73.4 percent-children,75.6 percent-grandchildren). He went on to say, *"In the past it was a given that children would enjoy better career and lifestyle opportunities than their parents. That chapter in American life appears to be ending."* Over 65 percent of respondents replied no when asked if they thought their children will be able to afford retirement. Over 70 percent doubt their grandchildren will be able to afford retirement.

A very wise man once said,

"There is nothing new under the son."

-King Solomon

The enclosed is a re-print of a 10-10-11 newsletter called Uncommon Wisdom produced by Weiss research reprinted with permission.

NOTICE THESE EVENTS WERE PREDICTED PRIOR TO 10-10-11

7 Major Advance Warnings

by Martin D. Weiss, Ph.D.

Monday, October 10, 2011

As soon as we see the likelihood of major bankruptcies and defaults, we don't wait around. We warn you immediately. We know you need time to get your money out of danger. And we also know that financial disasters don't obey any clock. They can strike suddenly — especially in the stock and bond markets, where investors often start selling in anticipation of the troubles to come. That's why we specifically warned our readers about:

- The failure of Bear Stearns 102 days ahead of time (Money and Markets of December 3, 2007) ...
- The failure of Lehman Brothers 182 days ahead of time (Money and Markets of December 3, 2007 and March 17, 2008)
- The near-failure of Citigroup 110 days before (Money and Markets of August 11, 2008)... · The failure of Washington Mutual 51 days before (Money and Markets of August 11, 2008), with advance warnings also issued many months earlier (Safe Money Report of March 2007 and June 2008) ...
- The demise of Fannie Mae four years before it collapsed (Money and Markets of September 24, 2004), plus .
- The failure of nearly every bank and insurance company that has occurred since Weiss Ratings began rating them, decades ago. Now, the time has come to issue new advance warnings — some of the most important in the 40-year history of my company. My new warnings are mostly focused on Europe. But as I'll explain below, they're bound to have a life-changing impact on nearly all investors in the U.S. and around the globe.

7 WARNINGS

Warning #1

Greece will default very soon

Banks and other investors who hold Greek notes and bonds have already seen massive losses in their market value — over 50 percent on two-year notes and even more on other issues. Until now, European authorities have turned a blind eye as their largest banks continued to carry these toxic assets on their books at full value — as if they were the best, most pristine assets in the world ... as if the sovereign debt crisis never happened! But now, European authorities are finally conceding that the banks must "partake in any solution of the crisis." In other words, the banks must bite the bullet and take some big hits in their Greek loans. They must officially recognize at least some portion of their losses. Conclusion: Whether the banks accept this "solution" voluntarily or not, it will mean Greece is in DEFAULT!

Warning #2

The contagion of fear will spread.

Anyone who thinks global investors will turn a blind eye to the Greek default is in for a big shock. Greece is not a small, third-world country. It's a member of the European Union and part of the euro zone. It has over 328 billion Euros in debt, more than Ireland and Portugal combined. Moreover, Greece is not alone, and investors know it. Investors will automatically assume — with good reason — that if one major Western government can default, so can others. And with that assumption, they will refuse to lend any more money to highly indebted governments. Or they will demand outrageously high yields.

Warning #3

European megabanks will collapse.

Some of Europe's largest banks will collapse under the weight of defaulting sovereign debts and in the wake of mass withdrawals. Spain's banks are especially vulnerable, swimming in a cesspool of bad mortgages left behind from that country's giant housing bubble and bust. In fact, this year, the European Banking Authority ran stress tests on the largest banks in Europe; and among the eight banks that failed the test, five were Spanish. Their names:

- Caixa Catalunya
- Unnim
- Grupo Caja 3
- Banco Pastor

Major French banks are bigger and in no less trouble. They barely passed the stress tests. And that was EVEN though they could cheat — not booking a penny of their losses on loans to Greece, Portugal or Ireland. According to Bankers Almanac, on a consolidated basis

- BNP Paribas has $2.7 trillion in assets, making it the largest in the world ...
- Crédit Agricole has $2.1 trillion and is the world's fourth-largest bank, and ...
- Société Générale has $1.5 trillion.

The total assets of these three French banks alone are greater than the total assets of the banking units of JPMorgan Chase, Bank of America and Citigroup. All three are drowning in bad loans to PIIGS countries. All three are in danger, in my view. But there's an even more imminent threat: mass withdrawals! You see, banks in the euro zone get less than 35 percent of their funds from deposits, according to Bloomberg data. Instead, they rely far more heavily on what's called "wholesale funding" — money borrowed from other banks and institutions. In other words, they're hooked on HOT MONEY! That's the kind of money that is quickly withdrawn at the first sign of trouble. And that's also the same kind of money that caused mass bank runs in the U.S. three years ago — runs that doomed big U.S. banks like Washington Mutual, while nearly sinking giants like Citigroup and Bank of America. Big European banks are especially vulnerable because they rely on hot money far more than U.S. banks. Therefore, the European Central Bank rushed to the rescue last week with 40 billion Euros in emergency loans for banks suffering withdrawals. But 40 billion is a drop in the bucket, barely covering ONE CENT for each dollar of PIIGS' debts outstanding. In the weeks ahead, will governments stand idly by while their biggest banks collapse?

Warning #4

European governments will suffer a cascade of new credit rating downgrades.

The richest governments of the European Union — France and Germany — will scramble to rescue their failing banks, and so, global markets may breathe a temporary sigh of relief. But recent history proves that the entire concept of bank bailouts is seriously flawed because of the following, now-obvious sequence of events: • In their zeal to save the banks and the economy, the governments gut their own fiscal balance. • They suffer big downgrades, losing their stellar credit ratings. • And as soon as they must borrow more money, they must pay through the nose with far higher interest rates. In other words, in their zeal to lift banks up from the brink of failure, the governments themselves are dragged down into the abyss. Case in point: Last week, we learned that Dexia, a Franco-Belgian megabank, is in distress. It's smaller than the giant French banks in trouble. But its assets are still 1.5 times the size of Belgium's ENTIRE economy! What happens if the government of Belgium tries to help rescue the bank? It will surely lose its still-good credit rating.

Indeed, late Friday, (10-7-11) Moody's announced it's ALREADY putting Belgium on review for a downgrade just based on the POSSIBLITY it may have to bail out banks like Dexia. Moody's specifically states that a key reason Belgium is on the ratings' chopping block is "the impact on the already pressured balanced sheet of the government of additional bank support measures which are likely to be needed." And the prospect of big bank bail- outs is also a key reason other major PIIGS countries have suffered massive downgrades in recent days. (More on this in a moment.)

Warning #5

Spain and Italy will be next to face default on their massive debts.

Spain and Italy have nearly $3.4 trillion in debt, or about 10 times more than Greece. But with their borrowing costs surging and their big banks failing, they will be unable to borrow enough new money to pay off old debts coming due. Result: Spain and Italy will also risk default.

Warning #6

Global debt markets will suffer a critical meltdown.

In anticipation of a default by a country as large as Spain or Italy, nearly all debt markets in the world will freeze, as investors withdraw in panic. This panic will not only crush the borrowing power of the PIIGS countries, hastening their default ... but it will also threaten to melt down the bond markets of countries like France, Germany, Japan, the U.K. and the U.S. That could mean sharply higher interest rates and, ultimately, the inability to borrow at almost any cost.

Warning #7

The vicious cycle of sovereign debt defaults and bank failures will lead to a global depression.

Sovereign debt defaults will trigger more bank failures. More bank failures, in turn, will precipitate more sovereign debt defaults. This vicious cycle will cut off the flow of credit to businesses and households, sink the global economy into a depression, and perpetuate the vicious cycle. Ultimately, we will see an extended period of great economic hardship for billions of people on every continent. Skeptical? If so, I don't blame you, and I assume you have your reasons. Yet there are far stronger reasons to be skeptical of all those who believe we can easily avoid disaster...

Reason #1

Even the highest authorities have admitted the dangers.

U.S. Treasury Secretary Tim Geithner warns of "cascading defaults," "bank runs," and "catastrophic risk." The International Monetary Fund says, "the global economy is in a dangerous new phase." World Bank President Robert Zoellick warns that Europe, Japan, and the U.S. are in such danger, they're threatening to *"drag down not only themselves, but the global economy."* And never forget: These statements are all from leaders who want to CALM financial markets! Imagine what they'd be saying if they were out of office and speaking freely! Clearly, the crisis has now progressed far beyond the deniability stage.

Reason #2

The major credit rating agencies have finally (and belatedly) begun to recognize the dangers.

Here are just a few of the most recent examples: This past Friday, October 6, Fitch downgraded Spain and Italy. Fitch cited the severity of the European debt crisis coupled with an increasingly recessionary atmosphere that can only impair governments' abilities to come to the aid of their faltering economies. On Spain, Fitch talked about the still sizeable structural budget deficit, high level of net external debt, and the fragility of the economic recovery as the process of deleveraging and rebalancing continues render the country especially vulnerable to such an external shock. For Italy, Fitch also stressed the *"high public debt and tax burden; an inefficient public sector; barriers to competition in product markets and services; inflexible labor market; and a pronounced north-south that a further worsening of the euro-zone debt crisis and volatility in the value of Italian government bonds will further erode confidence in the banking system. "In such a scenario,"* Fitch continues, *"concerns about the banks would start to weigh on the sovereign credit profile as a contingent liability and a vicious cycle of deteriorating sovereign and bank credit quality could emerge."*

The day before, on October 6, Moody's downgraded 12 U.K. financial institutions. The reasons? Like those cited for its earlier downgrades of major U.S. banks: Moody's believes that the U.K. government is now more likely to allow smaller institutions to fail if they become financially troubled ... and that even U.K.'s larger banks will suffer a reduction in the government's support. In other words, even if big banks fail, the government is likely to dish out less cash and more tough love. On Wednesday, October 5, Moody's downgraded Italy by three notches in one fell swoop. Moody's says Italy's ability to tap into sovereign debt markets may be constrained by the *"uncertain market environment and the risk of further deterioration in investor sentiment."* Alarmingly, writes IHS Global Insight, *"the rating agency also warned of further downgrades should any long-term uncertainty arise over the availability of external sources of liquidity support to Italy."* All told, including the downgrades of Citigroup and Bank of America announced the week before, we calculate that the countries and institutions downgraded in the last 10 days alone total at least $7.3 trillion in debts outstanding.

Reason #3

The era of big bank bailouts is over!

The facts are simple. Not even the richest countries of Europe could possibly afford to bail out their biggest banks. And conversely Not even the richest banks of Europe could possibly afford to finance the bulging deficits of their sovereign governments. Yet, right now, they are leaning on each other to avoid failing. European banks are holding on to the bad debts of sinking remnants are trying to find ways to keep the banks afloat. But this entire structure is based on nothing more than a pack of legalized lies: Banks can lie about the value of their loans to PIIGS countries, their capital and their solvency. And governments lie about how much it would really cost to save the insolvent banks. Solemn promises are made. Paper is shifted back and forth. But it's no better than rearranging chairs on the deck of the Titanic.

This Impacts You No Matter Where You Live

If you're a U.S. investor, you may think you're better off simply because the downgrade of the U.S. did not precipitate the feared collapse in U.S. Treasury securities. But that's merely due to a temporary flight to quality. Or if you're living in a country that's growing nicely and in good shape financially, you may think you're even more immune to Europe's crisis. But the European Union has the largest economy and the largest banks on Earth. It would be vastly unreasonable to think that Europe could fall and leave any other region standing. The market contagion ALONE would be enough to cause a global meltdown, destroying trillions of dollars in wealth in bonds, stocks and real estate. The big blows to corporate profits, trade and trust would merely compound those losses

So, my recommendations are unchanged:

- Get all or most of your money out of danger immediately.
- For any vulnerable assets you may still own, buy protective hedges — inverse investments specifically designed to rise when asset values fall.
- For funds you can afford to risk, go for potentially windfall profits, using those same inverse investments. And above all, stay safe!

Good luck and God bless!
Martin

7 WARNINGS

ABOUT:

Donald A. Galade, Financial Advisor

Donald A. Galade is President of Galade Financial Services, Inc.*, and CEO of GFS Financial Advisors, LLC, a registered investment advisory firm. GFS is an independent Registered Investment Advisor. Our mission is to provide the families and businesses we serve with innovative financial strategies, solutions, and planning that result in financial clarity and security.

At GFS, we believe no two investors are alike. In order to help each client meet their financial goals, we base our process on a client focused personalized approach using multiple investment strategies.

- Our advice and recommendations are tailored to our clients' investment goals, desired return objectives, risk tolerance, time horizon, cash requirements and tax situation.
- Our investment strategy is designed based on your long-term investment goals of preserving

principal, maximizing income or accumulating capital.
- As a fiduciary, we have an obligation to ensure the appropriate products are chosen based on the client's best interest.
- We develop your personalized asset allocation model based on individual risk tolerance, objectives and financial needs.
- Our goal is to maximize your investment returns while minimizing your risk through diversification of your assets.

Don has been in the financial services industry for more than three decades, serving families, non-profits, businesses and others in northeast Pennsylvania. Soon after he started his career, Galade recognized the need for resilient legacy plans. "I saw too many people unnecessarily put their retirement and legacy goals at risk."

He routinely attends intense training sessions that deal exclusively with financial needs of retirees and the latest strategies designed to meet those needs in retirement. He has written a book called, In God We Trust, In the Dollar We Worship, which is a narrative about what the Bible teaches us about money as it relates to his career as a financial advisor.

Also, he has served as a music director and an advisory board member of Faith Assembly of God Church in Hazle-Township, PA as well as Vice President of Pennsylvanians for Human Life, a former board member of Unico and is a former member of Kiwanis and Rotary clubs.

[1] Revelation 13:15

[2] Revelation 13:17

[3] Daniel 12:1

[4] 2 Corinthians 11:14

[5] Revelation 13:13

[6] Malachi Martin, The Keys of This Blood, A Touchstone Book published by Simon and Schuster ,1991, p.15

[7] http://nwo.syninfo.com/Crier/pcnwoqut.html

[8] Louise Branson Straits Times United States Bureau, Friday March 29, 2002.

[9] Phoebe Courtney, The CFR, Part II(Littleton Co:The Independent America, 1975),4

[10] The above article first appeared in the South-North Development Monitor (SUNS) of which

    Chakravarthi is the Chief Editor.

[11] Fidel Castro (no date)

[12] Cited Gary Kah, En Route to Glogal Occupation Huntington House Publishers 1992 p.41.

[13] Ellen WhiteTestimonies Vol.8 p.28

[14] Chandra Hardy ,Asia's Financial Crisis, Third World Network, Chandra Hardy is a retired senior economist of the World Bank.

[15] The above article appeared in New Dawn No. 34 (January-February 1996)

[16] Eric Toussaint is President of the Committee for the Cancellation of the Third World Debt (COCAD), and author of Your Money or Your Life, published in English by Pluto Press, London, 1999 and Vak, Bombay, 1999.

[17] Scott Latham, Market Opening or Corporate Welfare? "Results-Oriented" Trade Policy toward Japan

[18] Fidel Castro cited Third World Network. To access this site simply type in "Third World Network and

follow the links relevant to "economy" and "globalism".

[19] The New Republic Online. How Washington worsened Asia's crash. The Confidence Game. By Paul Krugman Issue date: 10.05.98 Post date: 09.17.98 Paul Krugman is a professor Of economics at MIT. [xxv][25] Sebastian Edwards, "The International Monetary Fund and the Developing Countries: A Critical

Evaluation," in Karl Brunner and Allan H. Meltzer, eds., IMF Policy Advice, Market Volatility, Commodity Price Rules and Other Essays (Amsterdam: North Holland, Autumn 1989), Carnegie-Rochester

Conference Series on Public Policy, p. 39.

[20] Economic Policy Institute, April 14, 2000 Issue Brief #142

[21] Interview with Kevin Danaher on Globalism and Its Discontents Policy.com

April 14, 2000 Kevin Danaher is co-founder of Global Exchange, and editor of the new book, Globalize This: The Battle Against the World Trade Organization and Corporate Rule

[22] Third World Network Globalisation weakens poor countries further by Gustavo Gonzalez

[23] Michel Chossudovsky is Professor of Economics, University Of Ottawa, and author of The Globalisation

of Poverty: Impacts of IMF and World Bank Reforms, Third World Network, Penang and Zed Books

www.ingramcontent.com/pod-product-compliance
Lightning Source LLC
Chambersburg PA
CBHW051319220526
45468CB00004B/1408